LIVE TO DIE

A JOURNEY IN DIVERSITY INCLUSION AND EQUITY

CAM STEWART

MIKOTSAPINUKUM (RED MORNING)

AR
PRESS

Library of Congress Control Number: 2025906670

Paperback ISBN: 978-1-966283-15-7
Hardcover ISBN: 978-1-966283-16-4

1. Main category— Books › Nonfiction › Politics & Social Sciences › Social Sciences › Discrimination & Racism
2. Other category— Books › Nonfiction › Politics & Social Sciences › Politics & Government › Public Affairs & Policy › Social Policy
3. Other category— Books › Nonfiction › Biographies & Memoirs › Leaders & Notable People › Social Activists

AR
PRESS

Published by: AR PRESS
Roger L. Brooks, Publisher
roger@americanrealpublishing.com
americanrealpublishing.com

TABLE OF CONTENTS

For all my relations

INTRODUCTION

WHEN I BECAME A CALGARY police officer, I did not foresee the way policing would change my perspective on crimes or incidents that go beyond burglaries, theft, damaging property, sexual and physical assaults, murders, drunk driving, and fraud. During the course of my law enforcement career, I was confronted with another spectrum of crimes where individuals were harmed—verbally, physically, psychologically, even financially—all based on their gender, race, colour, religion, sexual orientation or identity, or because of physical or mental disabilities. These crimes were not always obvious, and the victims were often too afraid to report them for fear of reprisal. There was a phrase I used in policing that helped guide my way: "Everyone counts, or nobody counts."

Then came the opportunity for me to be on the receiving end of a hate crime.

While operating as an undercover officer on Calgary's "gay stroll," an area where men went to meet other men for sex, I was robbed and assaulted. It was an incident I will never forget, because I wasn't a police officer in that skirmish. I was a victim who was presumed to be a gay man. So, I was the target of hate and bias. That event changed my life.

I suddenly became acutely aware of what it feels like to be a vulnerable person, one who is targeted with hate, bias and prejudice because of what they look like or who they love, not who they are as an individual.

When I began to confront perpetrators of hate and bias crimes as a police officer, I started my own deep journey into Diversity, Inclusion, and Equity, or what I like to call DIE. I think these words should be in this order—Diversity, Inclusion, and Equity (DIE)—as without Diversity and Inclusion, you will not get Equity. Also, the acronym DIE is easier to say and catchier too.

Over the last couple of decades, words to describe the work of social justice have morphed and changed many times. Several terms and ideologies have been popular, including race relations, cultural diversity, human rights, civil liberties, antiracism, diversity, inclusion, equity, belonging and welcoming. Three of these terms have been combined and used more in recent years: Diversity, Equity and Inclusion, abbreviated to DEI that most people are familiar with and has been adopted by many companies and organizations to articulate their commitment to eliminate bias and prejudice from their hiring practices. This work has its ups and downs, and the most recent backlash against "wokeism" is causing some companies and organizations to back away from DEI, and this is disconcerting.

I wrote this book to offer my stories, journey, and learnings to those who are interested in becoming advocates for people in our society who are on the receiving end of hate and bias crimes and racism. Even though I have a master's in intercultural communication, I have learned most of these valuable lessons in the field, sometimes the hard way. But as I pass them on to you, it is my goal to light a flame that will keep you motivated to walk the path of DIE, to become an advocate who makes a difference in your community and organizations, to be a lantern-bearer of light that overcomes places of darkness in our society.

We will start by recognizing how important it is to know our neighbours before we make assumptions about them. The only way to get to know our neighbours is to make the effort to do so, to initiate interactions, meet them where they are, to go to their events and be respectful of their differences from us. Becoming an open-minded and open-hearted person who works in the DIE space is challenging at times, but it is also extremely rewarding.

We will explore how to become people of action, people who have the courage to tackle thorny issues with empathy, good listening skills, and patience. A very important takeaway from this book is how *relationships are built at the speed of trust.* I have learned that over and over in my interactions with Indigenous people in Canada, with residents of the Cayman Islands when I went there to help with policing issues, and with middle-aged White guys in Rotary. DIE work is all about building relationships by developing trust.

While writing this book, I felt a need to develop some clear steps to DIE, so I came up with the system of Learning, Integrity, Valour and Engagement (LIVE). I believe you have to LIVE to DIE daily in your personal and professional life to truly master it.

When I retired from the Calgary Police Service, I knew I wanted to use my experience to advocate for fairness for newcomers, Indigenous people, Two Spirit, Lesbian, Gay, Bisexual, Transgender, and Queer (2SLGBTQ+) individuals, and people with disabilities. This is because I believe so strongly that our social fabric becomes threadbare if we aren't actively seeking to preserve it with the values of DIE. This led to my work as a corporate consultant, and for the Alberta Human Rights Commission.

My journey into DIE has taken me across Canada and internationally for speaking engagements and to deliver workshops, training presentations on a wide range of topics, including intercultural communication and conflict resolution. I have won local, provincial, national, and international awards for my work in fighting hate, racism, and discrimination. I have helped launch and advance nonprofit organizations that were created to provide awareness and training to people who want to make a difference in preserving and even healing the social fabric of their communities.

Why do I continue with this passion? Because I believe in change, transformation, and making the world a better, safer place for all our citizens. I can tell you that throughout my years working as a police officer, I saw the dark side of our communities. Towards the end of my law enforcement career, working in the DIE and human rights arena, I began to see the power of building relationships and promoting understanding and tolerance, and I found it is exhilarating to be part of positive change. I started my working life in the trenches within the criminal justice system and ended up fighting for justice and advocating for social justice.

I encourage you to read this book with an open mind, to think about the communities you are in, the groups you see are vulnerable, and notice the pockets of people who choose to act with hate and bias. I challenge you to ask what you can do to make things better. What are your strengths, gifts, and networks where you can leverage help, hope, and community-building actions that serve to reverse hate, racism, and discrimination?

At the end of each chapter, there are some "Food for Thought" questions to consider. You can advance your DIE awareness by writing down and thinking about your beliefs, values, and feelings towards these important subjects.

My hope is that the story of my journey in DIE will help you LIVE your journey.

In service and with heart,
Cam Stewart - Mikotsapinukum (Red Morning)

CHAPTER 1

KNOWING YOUR NEIGHBOUR

MOST PEOPLE HAVE HEARD OF DEI, which stands for Diversity, Equity, and Inclusion. Chances are the human resources department where you work crafted a corporate statement about how it honours DEI in its hiring practices, and that statement is on the company website too. Believe it or not, the origins of DEI can be traced back to the 1960s, when the civil rights movement was advocating for changes to society and the legal system.

Many people may perceive me as being "Male, Pale, and Stale." I don't know about the stale part, but as a middle-aged White guy, I get asked all the time how I got into this work and what is the process for others like me to join the ranks of being a Diversity, Inclusion, and Equity (DIE) advocate. My answer is that my path, like that of my colleagues in this area, was unique. It was both organic and with a focused intention. I joke half-heartedly that I have self-diagnosed ADHD (attention deficit hyperactivity disorder), in that I need variety and have trouble focusing on one thing. In this work, there is so much variety and there are so many opportunities to gain experience that you cannot focus on just one thing for a long time. We are unique beings, each with our own goals and dreams, and the journey is to find out what those are for our neighbours (customer, client, colleague, coworker...).

How did our society arrive at the need for DIE?

As our population becomes more diverse and less "one size fits all," it is a business and social imperative for us to understand and engage with those who do not look, act, learn or pray like us. For corporate and nonprofit organizations, this will increase access to employees, customers, volunteers, and investors, while decreasing lawsuits and human rights complaints, as well as loss in productivity and public confidence.

First inhabited by Indigenous people for thousands of years, Canada has grown to become a successful democratic nation with the original migration of people from primarily the European continent. Over the last fifty years, Canadian society has transformed dramatically, in large part due to changes in the demographics of our population. The change was inevitable, as government policy increased immigration levels in response to decreasing natural birth rates and to address the need for Canada to have a globally competitive workforce. Source countries of immigrants expanded to those from more continents and included those who came as refugees fleeing social, political, environmental, and economic problems. Canada's Indigenous populations, made up of First Nations, Inuit, and Métis people, have also seen an exponential natural birth rate growth after being decimated by European expansion, colonization, Indian residential schools, and the Indian Act.

In the 1970s and '80s, our country passed laws to protect individual rights, as well as to encourage institutional and personal responsibility. This included the Canadian Charter of Rights and Freedoms, the Human Rights Acts, and labour regulations. These have helped reduce discrimination and increase the workforce participation of Indigenous people, women, people with disabilities, people of colour, and those who identify as Two Spirit, Lesbian, Gay, Bisexual, Transgender, Queer, and other gender minorities (2SLGBTQ+).

Those who traditionally have power and influence have resisted these social and cultural changes. For many people, the golden days are gone when straight White men of European descent were in the majority and had control or influence over Canada's schools, companies, workforces, politics, and even recreation. Despite this opposition, leaders in government and wider society have removed barriers for those who previously did not have opportunities to participate equally in our society.

Much of this change and challenge to the status quo has been led by women, as well as those who identify as Black Indigenous and People of Colour (BIPOC) or different sexual orientation and gender diversity. Even with the shift in Canadian demographics, corporate, and nonprofit organizations, White people still dominate the leadership roles and staffing in workplaces. In the last few years, there has been a backlash, particularly from the White men in leadership, where we are seeing organizations step back from any diversity initiative gains that have been made. Yet the need for DIE in our workplaces, institutions, and nonprofits has never been more important than now, when our society is more diverse than ever.

Learning by Doing

Although I am a lifelong learner who has taken dozens of courses and has a graduate degree in intercultural communication, my preferred style of learning is kinaesthetic (learning by doing). As Don Vito Corleone said in *The Godfather*, "I have learned more in the streets than in the classroom." In my view, diversity work is not only an academic exercise, nor is it just about a human resources policies. Diversity work is a human experience. It is a way of truly seeing people who are different from you. We need to explore for ourselves the environment that we live in, in an interactive and firsthand way. This book will be a window into my experiences on how to DIE. Through my storytelling and encouraging you to practice several of my techniques, the hope is that you will be inspired to go down your own positive path and LIVE to DIE.

My writing style originates from more than forty years of writing police and government reports, where *Dragnet*'s

Sergeant Joe Friday would say, "Just the facts, ma'am." I have tried to stretch my abilities and dive into each subject more than usual to help uncover ingredients to DIEing better.

This book is for anyone who is interested in being a DIE advocate in their work or community environment, whether they are new to it or are already on a challenging journey. Community engagement specialists will also benefit from this information, as it will help them understand how to collaborate with people who are not from their background or community. I hope my unique experiences over the last twenty-five years as a baby boomer, able-bodied, White heterosexual male can inspire others to be our next leaders.

Allies and Edgewalkers

An ally is supportive and sympathetic to a different group of people. I have always been someone who does this, but I think a more accurate title would be "edgewalker." Tim Fox, vice president of the Calgary Foundation, introduced me to the concept of the edgewalkers' role in advancing equity issues, which resonated with me. From edgewalker. com, edgewalkers are described as "people who walk between worlds and can build bridges between different worlds. They have a strong inner life and are very grounded and effective in the everyday external world. They look to the future and focus on openness to possibilities." This could be anyone in your organization or community, or it could be you, especially if you are a:

- Leader
- Manager

- Coworker
- Engagement/partnership specialist
- Educator
- Parent
- Police Officer
- Politician
- Health worker

How did I become involved in DIE work?

I have written this book from my perspective as a White middle-aged man who has been engaged in diversity, inclusion, and equity (DIE) for over twenty-five years. My journey into DIE began when I spent five years leading work in the Calgary Police Service Cultural Resources Unit alongside some amazing officers—Martin Cull, Doug Jones, Don Muldoon, Shafik Punja, Tyler Stoutenburg, Sandy Tsuruoka, and Neville Wells—fully supported by Chief Christine Silverberg and Deputy Chief Rick Hanson. I spent five more years providing advice, training, and consulting services for corporate, nonprofit, and government organizations. Then I spent fifteen more years as a policy and program consultant for the Alberta Human Rights Commission, with our Communication, Education and Engagement team of Deborah Abiola, Nicholas Ameyaw, Gail Baron, Susan Coombes, Anne Clennett, Jasvir Chatha-Bains, Carolyn Ormsbee, Cassie Palamar, Jessica Snow, and Sushila Sami. We had seven chief commissioners during this time who each made a positive impact in the province, including Blair Mason, Robert Philp, William McFetridge, Michael Gottheil, and Kathryn Oviatt. All this experience has given me a policy and political view of our societal challenges and opportunities.

Over this time, I have learned that most of the resistance to this type of work comes from people who look like me and have been raised in a society where the systems have been developed to support men of European descent who are able-bodied and straight—or, as I say with a wink, "male, pale and stale." Our institutions (government, businesses, and places of worship) have a history of giving preference to White men and putting up barriers to others, including women, Indigenous people, people with disabilities, people of colour, and those identifying as 2SLGBTQ+.

One concept that has stuck with me over the years is the difference between the "Golden Rule and the "Platinum Rule." Most people know the Golden Rule as a universal concept of "treating people the way YOU would like to be treated." It turns out that almost all religions have this as an ethical code that is written in their scriptures. Growing up, my Christian bible told me to "Do unto others as you would have them do unto you" and "You shall love your neighbour as yourself." Among the many faith groups I came into contact with over the years, I learned that they had a similar belief, such as in Judaism, Jewish people learn "Never do to anyone else anything that you would not want someone to do to you." In Islam, Muslims believe that "None of you will believe until you love for your brother what you love for yourself," and people following Hinduism practice "Do not unto others that which would cause you pain if done to you." The Golden Rule is a great starting point for ethically working with others, but it assumes everyone around you has the same worldview and wants the same things in life. In our increasingly diverse workplace and group environments, we should be applying the Platinum Rule of "treating people the way *they* want to be treated." This concept requires more work as it puts a higher emphasis of understanding and respect of other people's differences. Anyone practicing DIE needs to understand and incorporate the Platinum Rule as they LIVE it.

This book is for anyone who is interested in being a DIE advocate in your work or community environment, whether you are new to it or already on your own journey. Community engagement specialists will benefit from this information, as it will help you understand how to collaborate with people who are not from your background. I hope my unique experiences can inspire others to be our next DIE leaders.

There is so much more work to be done. You can always DIE another day, but let's start today!

FOOD FOR THOUGHT:

1. Why are you interested in Diversity, Inclusion, and Equity—DIE? What's in it for you?

2. Where are you in your DIE journey?

3. What is your role in your organization, and how do you think you can advance DIE initiatives?

CHAPTER 2

"LIVE AND LET'S DIE."

ALTHOUGH DIE HAS PRIMAR-
ILY BEEN applied to employ-
ment issues, I have focused my efforts
on organizational change initiatives that
impact a variety of outcomes within
corporate, government, and nonprofit
sectors. This includes communication,
outreach, engagement, fund development, and education. Here is how I
understand the concept of diversity,
inclusion, and equity.

- **D – Diversity is a Fact.** It refers to the representation of a variety of people from diverse backgrounds
and lived experiences.

- **I – Inclusion is an Act.** It refers to how people feel
a sense of belonging and integration because of the
actions of society around them.

- **E – Equity is the Impact.** It refers to fair treatment and the allocation of appropriate resources and compensation for all people equally.

The *diversity* of humans is immeasurable. Among the billions of human beings on our planet, each of us is unique in many ways. Visibly, we can look different, whether it is the colour of our skin, hair, and eyes, or our height, weight, abilities, disabilities, or gender. We talk differently, with our language, accents, and pace of speech. It would take pages and pages to list all the physical differences present in humans. Then too, diversity goes beyond physical differences. It includes factors that are invisible. We have different learning, communicating, and cognitive styles as well as psychological disabilities, and all of these may change over time and be episodic. Sexual orientation can also make us unique, and this diversity may be visible or invisible. In many cultures or societies, people do not share or are uncomfortable sharing who they have sexual relations with, who they love, or to whom they were married.

Now think about *inclusion*. Even with the wide range of differences among humans, the social constructs of our societies try to group us into different nations, tribes, and groups. Also, the human condition is such that we all want to belong to a family, group, or team, as this gives us identity, pride, and sense of community. From the time we were kids on a playground, we have all wanted to be included in the games and groups. We prefer to gravitate and like people who look like us. I have a saying: "Like likes like." We like people who look like us and act like us. This is a bias that all of us should be aware of as we engage with others.

It has always surprised me how quick we are to *exclude* people from our organizations, our tribes, and our inner circles. It is unsettling that we want to differentiate and discriminate because we look, act, or believe in things differently. While there is benefit in enjoying our similarities, why does that have to be exclusive? Why can't we enjoy and share and benefit from the diversity all around us? How do we so easily lose sight of the interdependence we all depend upon for our survival and enjoyment of this thing called life?

The fact is that we need to see who is not being included in the conversation, what groups are not represented, and what the barriers for them are. These barriers can come from individuals or organizations, and they are likely systemic in nature. By actively looking for the barriers, our companies and organizations can address them to create a more inclusive and welcoming environment for all.

Here is a great quote that expresses the difference between diversity and inclusion. It comes from Verna Myers, vice president of inclusion strategy at Netflix:

> *"Diversity is being invited to the party.*
> *Inclusion is being asked to dance."*

And finally, *equity*. All of us just want to be treated fairly and equitably. We all want opportunities to use our skills and talents to show what we can do and accomplish our personal and professional goals. Each of us would like to participate fully in all that our organizations and society has to offer. If this is not available to us, there is a perception of lack of fairness that can grow like a cancer within the person or their community. Equity also means that not only do we remove the barriers, as we talked about with inclusion, but we also look at what we can do to support individuals to overcome any barriers that are in their way. This could mean providing extra support and mentoring that would compensate for not having any support. Or it could be a decision to consciously work with different populations and their leaders to promote and attract the best candidates from those communities to our organizations, clubs, and networks.

If you want to make a positive impact on society's right to DIE, you need to **LIVE** (Learn, Integrity, Valour and Engage).

- **L – Learn:** A deep dive into a culture that is not your own through listening, experience, and application
- **I – Integrity:** Having an honest, moral, and principled approach to how you work with others
- **V – Valour:** Being courageous, brave, and bold in all you do
- **E – Engage:** Actively look for ways to connect and collaborate with individuals and groups

DIE work cannot be an academic exercise or a "one and done" enterprise. Over the last twenty-five years, DIE has been pushed on organizations, their leadership teams, frontline staff, and management without talking with them and having conversations about what diversity, inclusion, and equity means to them and their institutions. Because it has been done poorly, there have been lots of pushback and resistance.

There has been an exponential growth in DIE work in recent years, since the death of George Floyd and the progress of movements like Black Lives Matter. The antiracism approaches to DIE have often polarized people and organizations, which has set back a lot of the positive work that was previously accomplished. This pushback can become an opportunity to reset the conversation and rethink why and how to DIE. Most adults learn best by doing, so I believe in this work you need to LIVE to DIE. We know that a one-hour online course or even a full-day, in-person workshop will not necessarily change a person's knowledge, skills, or awareness of any subject, especially one that is so complex and ingrained in our conscious and unconscious biases or organization systems.

Learning is Crucial

The Learn part of LIVE is the most important one. It is done by being open-minded, nonjudgmental and questioning one's own beliefs. Even if we look back at recommendations from Canada's Truth and Reconciliation Commission's calls to action, education and awareness are a focus of the truth part. It is important for people to have their own learning journey, and that means doing a deep dive into your own understanding of what DIE is and what things look like from your personal, family, and community's viewpoint. How are you different from or like other people in your circle?

After you have done that learning, it is also important to do a deep dive into different cultures and communities, particularly those you are working with or may work with that are not your own.

I am fortunate to be bicultural; I have worked and lived in other cultures and with people from other cultures. Every time I did, I took the time to learn about where that person came from, who their ancestors were, and what languages they spoke. Again, it is not about just looking at people as being a living library, but also about going to events and gatherings in that culture and community. It is learning through experiences and asking questions. You will more than likely make honest mistakes, and that is only human. Be present in your learning journey by using your head, heart, and hands.

I is for integrity and having an honest, kind, and morally principled approach to how you interact with others. This is extremely important, because people will know whether you are authentic and are there for the right reasons. Integrity may also be telling people that you are uncomfortable in a situation, but it is important to be honest, because Indigenous people, Black folks, and others who have been through colonization can smell BS from a mile away. Their ancestors were lied to, cheated, and taken advantage of by Western peoples. You will gain acceptance by being frank about what you know, where you stand on the subjects, and what you are prepared to do.

Valour is tied very closely to integrity. Being courageous, brave, and bold in DIE is not easy work or for the faint of heart. At times, you may have to talk truth to power and tell a leader or organizer that they have done something wrong, that they have not followed proper protocols, or that something offensive or illegal was said or done. This may not only be uncomfortable for you, but you might put yourself in a precarious situation. Hopefully, putting people on their heels does not challenge their authority and is done with integrity and knowledge that will lead to a learning opportunity for them and their organization.

In some situations, if you are a White person, you may have more power to bring things forward with less risk to your position, employment, or status than others in the community.

By being brave and standing up for justice, you may be viewed as a troublemaker, not a team player, or as someone who wants to rock the boat. Your courage will help you look in the mirror at the end of the day and be proud that you did the right thing.

"If you are neutral in situations of injustice, you have chosen the side of the oppressor. If an elephant has its foot on the tail of a mouse, and you say that you are neutral, the mouse will not appreciate your neutrality."
—Desmond Tutu

Calgary Fire Chief Steve Dongworth sat down with the Codey McIntyre, president of the Calgary Firefighters Association, a couple of years ago on a video and talked about how the best policies of the department were no good if the frontline staff and the people in the fire halls stayed silent. Both men said that addressing racism and discrimination was only possible if their brave people stood up for themselves and others when they witnessed improprieties. Valour is standing up for what you believe, in private or public, despite physical, emotional, or financial dangers.

E is for engagement. This means you will actively look for ways to connect and collaborate with individuals and groups. This is imperative to LIVE. For many people this is hard, especially if they are introverted or shy, but that can be overcome by joining smaller groups or putting themselves in situations where they are uncomfortable. We have all started a class or a job or joined a club where we did not know anyone, and we learned how and where we fit in. We did this by showing up, being present, listening, and asking questions. Then we identified what we could do and how we could support and advance the goals and dreams of the group. By getting to know people, we gain their trust and build relationships that we hope will be mutually beneficial for both us and those people or the communities we are reaching out to.

In this book, I will share my DIE experiences using LIVE as I explore the world of DIE. For the benefit of the reader, I will limit my examples, even though there are *A Million Ways to DIE in the West* (the title of a 2014 movie). My hope is that the lessons I have learned will benefit those entering the field or trying to build better communities and organizations. Each section will have LIVE applications for you to consider as you advance in your personal journey to DIE. As a big Trekkie (Star Trek fan), I think Captain Jean-Luc Picard said it best about this subject:

"LIVE now; make now always the most precious time. Now will never come again."

FOOD FOR THOUGHT:

1. Thinking back to the death of George Floyd in the US in May 2020, how did you feel about the Black Lives Matter protests that happened?

2. How have you used the LIVE principles of Learn, Integrity, Valour and Engagement in your work or home life?

CHAPTER 3

MY BACKGROUND IN THE WORLD OF DIE

MY MATERNAL GRAND-PARENTS IMMIGRATED TO Toronto, Canada, from Sebaa, Lebanon, where they had nine children. My mom, Delia Aziz, the youngest in the family, was born on a homestead farm in southern Saskatchewan. She divorced my dad, and I spent much of my early youth with my grandmother (Siti, in Arabic). I have such fond memories of growing up Lebanese and learning the culture, language, and especially the food (both making and eating it). I knew I looked different from the rest of my Aziz clan, but I always felt loved, and I happily remember the family photos where I was the "white sheep" in the mix, as my skin colour was lighter than everyone else's. Even though

I had the best extended family a boy could want or need, I still found ways to get into trouble and ended up on the wrong side of the law. Luckily, one of my many arresting officers took me under his wing, and I was invited/court-ordered to join an army cadet corp. This one act changed the direction my life was going and inspired me to serve my fellow citizens as a police officer, where I could aspire to help youth as I had been helped.

I was only a kid at twenty years old when I joined the Calgary Police Service in 1980. At six feet tall, with blond hair, green eyes, and the Scottish name of Cameron Stewart, I could pass as 100 percent WASP (White Anglo-Saxon Protestant). I later found out that that the Stewart side was actually Irish, but my grandfather told everyone he was Scottish to avoid the discrimination Irish immigrants faced at the time. I was excited and idealistic when I showed up for my first shifts in the east side of the city. In my mind's eye, I can still see my training officer driving around Forest Lawn, one arm out of the car, with a cigarette hanging out of his mouth, telling me how he was "not racist and treated everyone equal." I thought to myself, "Yeah right, equally bad." Then he went on to say that the worst part of his job was dealing with the "Lebs." This shocked me, as this was my ancestry and these were my people. I only had positive thoughts and perceptions of the Lebanese and Arabic community. But what could I say? I was young, new, and trying to fit into an organization and occupation that I had wanted so much, moved across the country for, and fought so hard to join. So, I said nothing; for many years I was a "closeted Lebanese." I saw first-hand what was happening to gay, female, Black, Asian, and Indigenous officers, and I did not volunteer to "out" myself. There were jokes, memes, and innuendos being told about them and in their presence. It was discomforting for them and for me, but for any of us to stand up would have been career suicide, literally.

Policing always has been and still is a male, White-dominated occupation, where terms like "brotherhood," "Back the Blue," and "Thin Blue Line" resonate with rank and file. I had observed firsthand instances when officers crossed a line, when they in good conscience said something or stood against a fellow brother-in-arms. It was known that if they did this, they could be posted to a less desirable role/unit, refused promotion, or even worse, not receive back-up at a dangerous call. During these years I still practiced my family traditions and made traditional foods for my family and true friends. I shared my background with colleagues I trusted, like Sat Parhar and Mike McNamara, and often found a sense of home with Lebanese members of the community. Looking back, I think as I grew older, my police family was feeling less safe for me to be my true self. I gained an appreciation for what female, gender-diverse, or visibly different officers were no doubt facing on a daily basis.

Over the years I have found my voice and learned to stand up for myself and those I see being bullied, harassed, or impacted by racism and discrimination. There are several strategies that I have used, but the most effective for me has been bystander intervention. There are also several methodologies, but the simplest is the 5-D approach: Distract, Direct, Document, Delay, and Delegate.

- **Distract** – Interrupt the incident by asking the victim some questions and ignoring the offender. Talk about something unrelated to what is going on.

- **Direct Action** – Identify and call out the perpetrator's behaviour. This is more effective if there are others in the vicinity, for safety reasons.

- **Document** – It is important to record and take notes of the incident. Seeing a mobile phone recording the altercation may cause the offender to stop the behaviour. Notes made at the time or shortly afterwards can be useful to prosecute and convict the offender of a criminal, human rights, or civil charge.

- **Delay** – Depending on the volatility of the situation and safety for all, it may be appropriate not to respond immediately to the incident. If this is the case, it is important to check in with the victim and see what support you can offer or they need.

- **Delegate** – Contact someone who has authority to address the situation. This could be a workplace supervisor, store manager, or law enforcement agency. This can be done with the agreement of the victim or by the witness alone.

During my law-enforcement career, I became more aware and accepting of my identity and of other people around me. In doing so, like minded sworn and civilian members gravitated towards me as my circle of friends and colleagues. I now know that this helped me define and advance my DIE journey. You are never too old to DIE!

LIVE Application

The first step on your way to DIE is to **learn** about yourself. This includes doing the work to understand your ancestry, communication styles, and how you prefer to resolve conflict. Most of us do not do the important inner work or try to figure out why we have discomfort around those who are different from us.

Are we honest with ourselves? Do we have the **integrity** to critically look at the previous actions of ourselves and our ancestors (parents, grandparents, etc.) in relation to how and why we acted in certain ways towards those who were not from our culture or looked different from us?

Valour and bravery are easier said than done. As humans we are wired to protect ourselves and our kin first and worry about others later. DIE work requires that we put our own needs and safety aside sometimes. This dissonance may be emotionally and mentally challenging at first.

I have found that you must **engage** with those who are like-minded as well as those who have different views from yours. This will help you understand all sides of the conversation and why people think and act in certain ways.

FOOD FOR THOUGHT:

1. What is your DIE (Diversity, Inclusion, or Equity) story? How did your ancestors have struggles in migration, settlement, or integration?

2. How many of your friends and family are supportive of you doing DIE work?

CHAPTER 4

RELATIONSHIPS ARE BUILT AT THE SPEED OF TRUST

Like most people in Canada, I grew up with very little knowledge of Indigenous people or their history, outside of what I saw in media, learned in school, or experienced firsthand. When I joined the law enforcement community at the age of twenty, I was prepared to learn about all the communities we served, but little positive information was taught or shared about Indigenous people. Unfortunately, as a police officer I only had interactions with Indigenous people who had substance abuse problems or were offenders or victims in the criminal justice system The comments and actions of my colleagues and senior officers only reinforced and promoted negative stereotypes. I must admit that these interactions, combined with my limited knowledge, impacted my perception of Indigenous people.

At one point in my career, while working patrol downtown, I found myself thinking derogatory thoughts about the homeless Indigenous people I was encountering, and I had the urge to treat them with less care and humanity. I felt like I was losing my humanity and love for fellow humans. Having these feelings forced me to ask for a transfer, as I did not like how this working environment was impacting my approaches to fellow citizens. As a White man, I know I had privileges to be able to walk away from this toxic environment that many others may not have. Had I stayed, I know I would have learned to be more discriminatory towards Indigenous members of our community.

Later in my police career, I attended an Aboriginal Justice Camp hosted by Reg and Rose Crowshoe of the Pikani Nation, where I had interactions with smart, sober, and insightful elders and knowledge keepers. It was there that I realized how far my perceptions and negative stereotypes about Canada's first peoples influenced my actions and the outcomes they experienced. It was at this time that I decided all Canadians, including me, needed to reflect upon our relationships with Indigenous people. Determined to correct mine, I took a personal journey to meet with people and elders, as well as to attend Canada's Truth and Reconciliation Commission events. I learned of the history of residential schools, systemic discrimination, and the ongoing impacts these have had on current Indigenous youth, families, and communities.

While doing my master's program in intercultural communication, I decided to do my thesis on hate crime and incidents in Alberta. I travelled around the province asking individuals and groups from diverse and marginalized communities about their experiences related to discrimination, racism, and hate. One key finding, which was not found anywhere in previous research, was that Indigenous people experience hate and racism more than any other group in the province, while conversely, they are the least likely to report these occurrences to police, human rights commissions, or any other government body.

The personal stories I heard broke my heart, such as young Indigenous women being verbally and physically attacked, with their elders telling them to put their heads down and take it, as there was no support from the system. The Cree people have a word for this, "Kiem." This shocked me and added to my resolve that society needed to address these issues right away. This research and my thesis helped to inform and inspire my reconciliation work in Indigenous communities.

When I started with the Alberta Human Rights Commission, I requested to lead its engagement work with Indigenous communities in the province. I attended many events across the province, including community gatherings, round dances, and powwows. I listened to many of the testimonies of people who attended Indian residential schools at the Truth and Reconciliation Commission (TRC) hearings and participated in the 2014 regional gathering in Edmonton, where politicians of all stripes committed to reconciliation efforts. In 2015, with the release of the TRC report, with its ninety-four calls to action, I immediately engaged Reg and Rose Crowshoe to provide off-site training for all commission staff in Calgary and Edmonton.

As I participated more and became active with Indigenous groups like the Calgary Urban Aboriginal Initiative and the Calgary Indigenous Human Rights Circle, which were supported by inspirational people like Christy Morgan, Monique Fry and Tim Fox. I was called upon to provide advice and find resources for projects. I knew I was accepted in the community when I was presented with an eagle feather at a large community gathering by Elder Doreen Spence. This important item has immense meaning in traditional culture, where it is given to someone who shows bravery and dedication to the community, and I have always held it close to my heart as I continued to do this work. I broadened my understanding of the culture by learning about traditional spirituality and practices. I attended sweats hosted by several elders and committed to four vision quests (four-day fasts with no food or water). The vision quests, in particular, changed my life and transformed how I view my presence and role in the world, and I now consider Indigenous spirituality to be my "religion." During one of the fasts, I learned that my spirit animal is a wolverine. Wolverines are associated to being assertive, as they speak out and stand up, always staying true to oneself. My journey in Indigenous spirituality was made possible with the support and prayers of many people, including Rob Clarke, Shelly and Mark Morin, Rafael de la Pena, Don Shirley, Dr. Michelle Scott, and Allan Vonkeman. One of the things I sometimes get challenged with is the concept of *cultural appropriation*, or adapting Indigenous culture without respect or consent. I address this by saying that I have *cultural appreciation*, as I have been given the lessons by respected elders and earned the rights to use certain practices and protocols. Whenever possible, I co-present with Indigenous knowledge keepers and do not use the information that I have been gifted for personal gain.

As an ally to the community, I was often the only male, pale, and stale person at events or invited to sit on Indigenous working groups. I think that even though I was warmly welcomed, there may have been some people in the room who were nervous about my presence and waited for me to leave with their knowledge. I was on the Calgary Police Service Round Dance Committee since its inception in 2010. For the 2020 event, I was bestowed an honour that relatively few White people receive. In the presence of over 500 people, including my friends and family, I was gifted the Blackfoot name of Mikotsahpinukum, meaning "Red Morning," by Siksika Elder Herman Yellow Old Woman. He honoured me with the name of one of his ancestors, who would get up in the mornings and pray to the rising sun and red skies, asking for safe journeys, harvests, and battles. I believe this name was chosen to provide me with support and guidance as I go into new battles and journeys. Unlike a lot of awards or acknowledgments I have had, I use the name daily. It provides me strength and guidance to advance reconciliation efforts.

Back to the commission…. Now having this knowledge and expertise, I started changing the way the organization provided grants and supported Indigenous-led projects. Over a ten-year period, the Human Rights Education and Multiculturalism Fund went from granting less than one-quarter to granting half of its funds to Indigenous-led projects. We developed an honorarium policy to equitably compensate elders and knowledge holders who provide services to the organization, made a smudge box available in our Calgary office, and hosted weekly smudges for those who wanted spiritual support. After hosting numerous training sessions, as well as meetings with staff and Indigenous leaders, I drafted the commission's Indigenous Strategy, which was implemented in 2020. An Indigenous Advisory Circle was started with twelve amazing leaders from across the province who helped inform and direct the strategy. With advice from the Circle, ceremony protocols were included along with Western ways of thinking in how we operated. Two eagle feathers were gifted to the commission, and they were blessed by Elders Clarence Wolfleg and Howard Mustus Sr. in a ceremony on kihcih-kaw askî-Sacred Land in Edmonton. These eagle feathers are being used in commission meetings and complaint consolation efforts. At this ceremony, the strategy was also consecrated in a traditional pipe ceremony, which was attended by many of the staff and leadership of the organization. The Alberta Commission was the first in the country to do any of these things, and this has led to increased trust and confidence in the community.

When I started this journey twenty-five years ago, I thought it would be as simple as going into a community, making a few contacts, and voilà—we can fix things. I was frustrated many times at the setbacks and time it took to get things done. Blackfoot Elder Cassie Eagle Speaker had to remind me that *relationships are built at the speed of trust.* Canada's Indigenous relations have had many generations of bad faith negotiations, failed programs, underfunding, and mistrust. Government organizations, churches, academic institutions, and well-meaning White people have not had a good track record in Indigenous communities. They have come in with agendas and colonial ideas and have often left things worse off than when they came.

I was invited to a board meeting of an Indigenous organization that we funded, and an elder I did not know challenged me, "Cam, are you going to tell us what we can do with these project funds?" I replied, with a smile, "As a representative of Her Majesty Rachel Notley [who was the premier of Alberta at the time], I will only remind you of what you received the grant for and provide advice on how your programs will be seen by other funders." Everyone chuckled and realized that, as the *Toy Story* song goes, "You've got a friend in me."

As I go down this path, I have had to learn to slow myself and my organization's outlook on what can be meaningfully done in a prescribed time frame. Most Western, non-Indigenous systems have one-to-three-year planning cycles and try to measure their output and outcome indicators within this timeframe. Similarly, funders and philanthropic organizations fund projects this way as well. Indigenous and other collective communities operate under relational and holistic systems that take time and are often hard to measure. There are ways we can work within these competing systems by understanding others' worldview and building relationships.

We have all been in a relationship with a trusted best friend, partner/spouse, or family member. Working with communities has common values to personal relationship building of being humble, empathetic, open-minded, accountable, and committed to learn. Most importantly, I have learned relationships take time and energy. I do not go into them without thoughtful consideration. Here are some phases to building trusting relationships with Indigenous and other equity-seeking communities....

- **Courtship** – Sometimes you can call up an elder or community member to ask for a meeting, but that may feel like going on a blind date. It is often better to meet through a trusted third-party navigator who can facilitate the discussion. Alternatively, invite yourself or get an invitation to a community event where you can connect with individuals in person. Connecting with people takes time and consistency. It is important to be present and not wanting to rush off to your next meeting. Coffees, board meetings, and gatherings will take longer than you may be used to.

- **Bonding** – Find a reason to be connected and in a relationship. Work together to find the mutual benefits of this relationship or kinship. This can be done by identifying aligning goals and aspirations for both parties. For Indigenous peoples, priorities would include community, family, youth, elders, and the land/environment.

- **Commitment** – Make relationship building a priority throughout your engagement with this community and individuals. This should be the first objective, and it should be maintained throughout any initiative. The community needs to know that you and your organization are committed to long-term relationships. They have had their share of short-term "bad dates" in the past. We older folks might remember Humphrey Bogart saying in *Casablanca*, "This is the beginning of a beautiful relationship."

- **Partnership** – In any successful relationship, the partners need to have equivalent status (note that I did not say "equal"). The parties come with different ideas, backgrounds, skills, and resources that they can draw upon. For instance, Indigenous knowledge and connections may be more valuable than the financial contributions of a mainstream funder or partner. Ideally, any project or initiative should be Indigenous-led with their perspectives and ideologies being the foundation for the relationship. Your role should be as a friend, listener, adviser, collaborator, or advocate.

Cree Elder Dr. Doreen Spence OC taught me the lessons of "Wahkotawin," where we are in a relationship with every being on the planet. To be in this state, we need to build healthy relationships that lead us from the spaces in our heads to our hearts. This work must be done with "Kesewatisown" (love and kindness), doing whatever it takes for the betterment of all our relations.

LIVE Application

When **learning** about Indigenous culture, it is important to understand their true history (including before and after colonization), cultural and spiritual practices, and the current realities their community is facing. Some of this can be done by attending courses, reading articles, and watching movies. These are great safe ways to start your learning journey, but they should be supplemented with interpersonal and interactive methods. These include meeting with leaders, educators, and members of the community, attending gatherings and events, and participating in religious/traditional celebrations.

If you are honest and come to the community with a good heart and **integrity**, you will be in a better position to gain their trust. Try your best not over promise or under-deliver but be straight about what you or your organization may be able to contribute or do in different situations.

Valour is described in *Merriam-Webster's Dictionary* as "strength of mind or spirit that enables a person to encounter danger with firmness and equates this to personal bravery." Now is the time to DIE! Be brave—a **valorous** leader in your community or organization. You will not regret being at the forefront of DIE initiatives.

Engagement is the most important key in DIE. Too often people show up to one or two meetings, never to be seen again. Identify diverse ways and locations to connect where you can see what is happening and be seen in community. It is understood that you need to be "present" in these situations by paying attention and not being distracted by outside stimuli.

FOOD FOR THOUGHT:

1. Do you know the true history of Indigenous peoples? Take some time on the internet to do research and some myth busting.

2. Think of a time that you were an ally to someone or a group of people. What did you do then, and what would you do differently today for a better outcome?

CHAPTER 5

FOLLOW THE PATH LESS TRAVELLED – CROSS YOUR HEART AND HOPE TO DIE

A S A SEASONED INVES-TIGATOR WITH many important files to manage, I had little time for the mandated diversity training being taught in the 1990s. That was the consensus of most of the police rank and file. I believe many of my fellow officers did not learn much or use the lessons from those training sessions. Begrudgingly, I attended the last one-day course offered, but once I was there, I took it all in. As a lifelong learner, I realized that all training taught me the soft skills, important in any occupation, of working with other cultures. In policing, I was able to add those skills and lessons to my tool belt. Just like a gladiator putting on his armour, I put those DIE tools in my duty belt, along with the radio, handcuffs, and weapons.

It was not until a couple of years after this course that I was able to put one of the lessons to use. As a uniformed patrol officer, I was dispatched to a disturbance in a local gurdwara (Sikh temple). When I arrived, I saw groups of men at the front of the prayer hall fighting over a microphone. I took off my shoes, donned a head covering, and approached them. I was able to persuade them to leave the area and join me in the foyer for a conversation. Over the next hour, I de-escalated the conflict, but I knew there was much more going on and that it would not be long before things grew into violent confrontations. I went back to the station and tried to get support and advice from some of the officers and supervisors who were working in the patrol area where the temple was located. I got little or no help from them, and there were a few who said, "It is not our problem, we should let them kill each other." I continued to work with the warring parties, but I could see there was little movement, so I met with the elders, women, and youth (including future MLA Manmeet Bhullar). With their support and prodding, the men on both sides of the conflict came to a truce for the betterment of the community. I learned a lot about intercultural conflict resolution and communication styles during this case. It challenged my mind and attitudes so much so that when an opening came up in the Cultural Resources Unit, I jumped at it. I spent the next five years connecting and building bridges with the South Asian and Middle Eastern communities, as well as taking on the role of diversity training instructor for the department.

As there is a high percentage of South Asians in the northeast quadrant of Calgary, the district commanders of these districts asked me to provide training to their sworn and civilian staff. During one of these sessions, a team sergeant shouted out an offensive and racist joke. I immediately stopped my presentation and asked the officer to join me outside. Once there, I walked with him to the inspector's office, where the sergeant said, "Hey, Cam, we are friends, we play soccer together, and it was just a joke." I replied, "Those officers in there are under your care and they look up to you. There are South Asian officers in this district, some of your officers may have friends or relatives from that community. What kind of an example are you setting?" The inspector reprimanded the sergeant, and he went back into the room and gave a heartfelt apology to the class. Unfortunately, my relationship with the man ended on that day, as he never forgave me for outing his inappropriate humour and racism.

After several years of working with the Sikh community, I was approached by one of the leaders who told me his father, along with many of the elders, was afraid to go out in public or take public transit. There was a rash of incidents in northeast Calgary where elderly Sikh men were approached by young White men who stole or knocked off their turbans. When I spoke to a couple of the victims, they said they had called the police, and each time the officers said they would drive around the area, but they never bothered to take a statement or submit a report. I went back to the office and found that there had been a dozen similar occurrences dispatched to officers within the previous year. None of the officers considered that these were possible hate-motivated crimes. The crimes were robbery and combining assault with the thefts. As a hate crime, these offences were message crimes that polarized and stigmatized the community. I approached the district commander for this patrol area with my concerns about these cases, and he immediately assigned his best investigators. In short order, they interviewed the victims, collected evidence, and arrested several suspects. They learned that the offenders were a small gang who used the robberies to initiate new members.

When you are in the field of DIE, you need to walk the talk, meaning the necessity of not just teaching the subject matter but also living it. When I started working in this area, I was shy about challenging the status quo, be it an off-colour remark, an inappropriate email, or a discriminatory hiring policy. I realized, though, that if not me, then who should stand up to this kind of injustice? Can I look at myself in the mirror and be proud of how I reacted to situations that negatively impact communities that do not have a voice in the justice system? If this is my true calling, what do I have to lose? With twenty years of service, the worst they can do to me is send me back to patrol (and as far as I was concerned, that was one of the bests jobs in the department). So, I decided it was time to champion change in policing without regard to how it could impact my professional or financial outcome. I know this affected my mobility with the service, which I often reflect upon.

LIVE Application

Being new to police culture, I had to LIVE it to advocate for DIE. After twenty-five years in this industry, it was important for me to **learn** as much as possible about the people and institutions. No officer ever joined a department to be prejudicial or discriminatory; they joined to "serve and protect." The bias and fear of "others" joining their ranks was standard practice at all levels of the police service.

I know that many officers were uncomfortable with the status quo of what they saw or experienced. They witnessed a disintegration of **integrity** in their organization. There was not only bias shown towards other officers (female, 2SLGBTQ+, Indigenous, and people of colour), but it often was exponentially worse to civilian employees and volunteers who identified with those groups. Those officers who had integrity and brought forward concerns of others being treated inequitably were vilified, and their careers were not advanced. On the flip side, these same officers were successful in building bridges and relationships with equity-seeking groups on behalf of their agencies. This kind of retribution has become less prevalent in recent years, but it still happens.

Standing up and "serving and protecting" all citizens sometimes take guts and **valour**. It is not for the faint of heart, as you often must do some mental gymnastics to assess your physical and emotional safety. Even after being out of policing for twenty years, I still hear stories of courageous actions of officers bringing incidents forward and police officers being found negligent in human rights cases. True valour is knowing when to retreat, regroup and return stronger than ever—Price of Valour.

Through my career in law enforcement, I have found that you must **engage** with officers and department leaders with an understanding of their mandate and the challenges of the job. It is important to identify ways to layer DIE initiatives within existing policing strategies and priorities and not separate this work as an add-on to their workload. Police hostage negotiators use the mantra of "Time, Talk, and Tear gas" to resolve incidents; in DIE policing I suggest we use "Time, Talk, Tea, and Tears" to build trusting relationships and communities.

FOOD FOR THOUGHT:

1. When a friend, family member, or work colleague made a racist comment, what was your response? If you could have a do-over, what would you do or say now?

2. Think of a time when you witnessed discrimination in your workplace or community. With hindsight being twenty-twenty, how would you react to that situation today? What are some options that you could have said or done that may have been a teaching moment for the offender or a healing opportunity for the victim of the discrimination?

CHAPTER 6

WHAT TO DO ABOUT HATE CRIMES – THE MAD HATER

IN 2001, AS THE MIDDLE East police liaison officer, I saw firsthand the ugliness of hate and bias after the attacks on the World Trade Center by radical Muslim terrorists, done in the name of their religion. Canadians who were Muslims or looked like they followed Islam were targeted with extreme prejudice. Violent assaults against persons and property occurred, and Muslim community members feared for their safety. In the workplace, people lost their jobs, and many others were denied access to positions, especially in law enforcement. During this time in my career, I also got the opportunity to work closely with the Jewish community and see firsthand the impact of current-day antisemitism and hate towards people following Judaism.

After retiring from law enforcement, I was commissioned by the Alberta Hate Crimes Committee (AHCC) to write a major report on the status of hate and bias crimes in the province of Alberta. The report, "Combating Hate and Bias Crime and Incidents in Alberta," was released in July 2007.The Alberta Association of Chiefs of Police actively participated in this committee and supported the research and findings.

About the Alberta Hate Crimes Committee

The AHCC was conceived as a response to hate crimes and incidents that occurred in Alberta after the September 11, 2001 attack on the World Trade Center in New York. The committee organizers, Amal Umar from Canadian Heritage and Doug Jones from the Calgary Police Service, envisioned a coordinated provincial approach to hate crime investigation, intelligence, and community involvement. The committee's goals were to:

- Create public awareness and education programs.
- Develop partnerships to provide and gather information.
- Offer support for victims of hate crime.

Alberta law enforcement was having difficulty keeping up with the growing numbers of hate crimes in the province, and that is what prompted this report. My research involved interviewing police officers, judges, lawyers, Crown prosecutors, community leaders of minority and racialized groups, and government officials at the federal, provincial, and municipal levels. I also interviewed individuals who had been victims of hate and bias crimes. When I investigated the federal criminal code and rulings by the Supreme Court of Canada on hate crime cases, I came across this important quote from the court:

> "Hatred is predicated on destruction, and hatred against identifiable groups therefore thrives on insensitivity, bigotry, and destruction of both the target group and of the values of our society. Hatred in this sense is a most extreme emotion that belies reason: an emotion that, if exercised against members of an identifiable group, implies that those individuals are to be despised, scorned, denied respect, and made subject to ill treatment on the basis of group affiliation." (Supreme Court of Canada, R. v. Keegstra, 1990)

While in Fort McMurray, when I asked Black Muslim leaders if there was racism or hate in their community, they said there was not, but there was mainly "nepotism," where the White people were looking after their own kin first. Some thought this was okay, as back home they would protect the jobs for their countrymen first as well. In rural Alberta, my interviews found that many gay men and the businesses that supported them were targeted with violence, while conversely police did not have any reports of hate against this community. I learned that the reported hate crimes were either minimalized by law enforcement or intentionally ignored.

The groups I discovered that faced the most hate and bias crimes after the September 11 attack were Arabs and Muslims, Indigenous people in Alberta, and members of the 2SLGBTQ+ community, especially trans individuals. I also found that in some instances, when police were called in response to hate crimes, they didn't respond well or respond at all. Only the two largest policing agencies in Alberta collected hate-crime data at the time. Clearly there was room for police departments province-wide to take hate crimes more seriously in order to reduce them.

My report presented three major recommendations:

1. Creation of an Alberta Hate Crime Team that would report to the solicitor general's department.

2. Creation of an Alberta Hate Crime Committee.

3. Developing a Public Awareness Program of hate/bias crimes.

After completing the report, I stayed active in this field, being an adviser and later the president of the AHCC. I am happy to say there has been progress in Alberta fighting hate and bias crimes since the report was released. Police departments in Alberta's two largest cities, Calgary and Edmonton, have designated hate crime positions. The Alberta government has introduced a Provincial Hate Crimes Unit, and the AHCC has flourished, recently changing its name to STOPHATEAB and developing several public awareness and prevention programs. I am so proud to be a part of this organization, which is currently being guided by a strong executive director, Nina Saini, and an amazing board of directors.

So, what does this have to do with DIE?

A lot actually. When you look at the pyramid of hate, hate actions go from mental bias, prejudice, and discrimination to violence and genocide. If you are working in a role to promote DIE, you need to understand what happens when these crimes occur, and which resources exist to combat hate and support the victims. These crimes can occur anywhere—in workplaces, in public spaces, in schools, on public transit. Do you know what to do or how to support the victim if you witness a hate crime or incident?

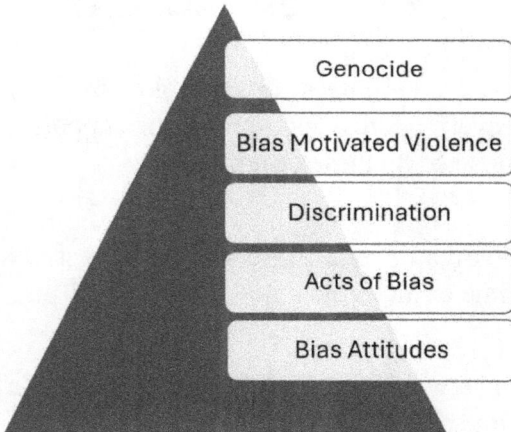

From BC Human Rights Commission

Our work to promote and ensure DIE does not occur in a vacuum, and our governments, police forces, and other stakeholders play a crucial role in responding to hate crimes and incidents.

FOOD FOR THOUGHT:

1. What committees or agencies in your city actively address hate crimes or support people impacted by these occurrences?

2. Have you ever experienced or witnessed a hate crime or incident?

3. What would you do if you witnessed a hate crime or incident?

CHAPTER 7

QUEEN OF CALGARY

A**S A POLICE OFFICER**, I was quite good at investigating, and I was drawn to files that involved people who were from different backgrounds and who were challenging. Luckily for me, most officers did not want to take on these cases, as they pushed them outside of their comfort zones. I took the C-train transit system to work one afternoon, and I overheard a group of males plotting to lure men who were looking for gay sex and rob them on Calgary's gay stroll. They knew these men would not report these crimes to police for fear of family humiliation and justice system apathy. I knew the gay stroll area well, as it was in my patrol area, and I had spent many shifts getting to know community members who identified as 2SLGBTQ+, as well as their places of congregation.

When I got to work, I told the duty sergeant what I had witnessed and overheard. It took a fair bit of convincing and arm-twisting to get his approval to investigate these offences that were about to be committed. Luckily, it was a slow night for dispatch calls, and I quickly put together an undercover operations plan and team made up of several young officers who were on shift. There were very few officers on that day who had surveillance training, so after several failed attempts to draw out the criminals, I went to the area acting as a man looking for gay sex. I was flagged down by one of the gang's leaders from the train. He got in my car, and we started to negotiate a deal. When I took out my wallet, he grabbed it and tried to run away. We got into a fight, and his cohorts came to help him, but little did they know that my team was just around the corner. The cavalry came to arrest them all in one swoop. I got a couple of cracked ribs during the altercation and had to take some time off work.

When the case was brought to trial, the prosecutor, in the traditional "Let's Make a Deal" fashion, tried to convince me to drop some of the charges. I was surprised that this clear-cut case targeting a marginalized population was so quickly being downgraded and minimized. I refused adamantly. As the victim and arresting officer, I knew this was a solid case of hate-motivated crime (assault and robbery) and the offenders should receive the appropriate sentencing.

After investigating this crime and bringing it to a successful conclusion, which was covered extensively in the media, I was interested to see the differences in response. From my fellow police officers, I was nicknamed "the Queen of Calgary" in a derogatory fashion, and the department did little to applaud my investigation or case management efforts. I was shocked that my brothers in blue would be so crass and homophobic by downplaying these types of hate crimes. They made me feel humiliated about helping a marginalized community. One part of me wanted to lash out at them, and the other part wanted to avoid causing any problems by following their line of thinking On the flip side, the 2SLGBTQ+ community acknowledged my efforts in their community newspapers, and I received many letters from their leaders while I was recovering saying they were extremely pleased that police department had finally acted on this kind of criminal activity that had long been a reported but remained an unaddressed issue affecting their community.

LIVE Application

Having taken the time to **learn** about 2SLGBTQ+ culture proved invaluable for me to understand their motivation for not reporting crimes against them and why they are a target for unscrupulous offenders. Even though I was not from that community, I could empathize with their issues and needs and looked at how to support them.

It was important for me to have **integrity** when the case came to court. The easy and timely out would be to agree to the deal the prosecutor and the defence were cooking up. Luckily, I was prepared and could articulate the strengths of the case and the value to society for an appropriate conviction and sentence.

Valour is an asset in policing, but often one must go above and beyond. It is frustrating, though, when you must be bold within your own ranks, organization, and those who are there to support the wheels of justice. It is extremely satisfying when your courage pays off with righteous results.

There is a well-known quote by Edmund Burke: "The only thing necessary for the triumph of evil is for good men to do nothing." To practice DIE you must **engage** with the issues as they arise and not turn a blind eye. Silence or inaction only makes the situation worse.

FOOD FOR THOUGHT:

1. What are you comfortable to do when learning how to build bridges with people who are vulnerable minorities?

2. Think of a time when you used your voice to speak up for someone else. How did you feel?

3. How would you feel if someone spoke up for you or your community?

CHAPTER 8

THE NEW CENTURION

As a typical White guy and police officer of my generation, I was a fan of action and police films. Many years ago, I watched the classic 1970s movie *The New Centurions*, and there was a scene in the locker room where the rookie and his senior officer were discussing their role in policing. Like the Centurions, the guards for the Roman Empire, they were guards for the new empire in New York City. As they donned their cop uniforms, they could notice the change in their demeanour and attitudes. This scene struck a chord with me, because when I put on each piece of my police uniform, I could feel a change in my posture, presence, and perceptions. I realized that my centurion uniform and chariot (a patrol car) gave me a sense of power and invincibility, while at the same time they created a barrier between me and the community that I was there to serve. I saw "discrimination" being hidden under the umbrella of "discretion," and I had to make efforts consciously and consistently to be less centurion and more Citizen.

This turned out to be harder than I expected, as there were protection and power in staying in this role. It was often emotionally and physically safer to wear the armour (on and off duty). Getting out of work was easier than getting work out of your head. Over time, though, I began shedding this sheathing and let down my guard. Taking off each piece of equipment and not indiscriminately using my titles, position in society, and designated powers allowed me to engage authentically with the community. I could sense there was a positive change in me that helped me be a better police officer, community member, and father. In living DIE, I have learned that you must not only know your power and privilege, but you must know when to humbly take it off and come down to earth.

When I went from working in the criminal justice field to the social justice area of addressing human rights, discrimination, and racism, there was less armour available to defend myself. Although the dangers were just as real, I worked long hours to protect our citizens from discrimination and racism. There was very little support from the organizations or colleagues. At the same time, there was a growing trend and pushback in society against advancing newcomer integration, women's advancement, Indigenous reconciliation, and 2SLGBTQ+ inclusion. The scars of hearing the stories from victims while listening to public apathy added to any vicarious or real trauma I had experienced. I am not sure if it being a male, or a male in a female-dominated sector, is why I did not seek out help or made a conscious decision to internalize and hide the pressure I was feeling.

Doing the DIE work, I often felt like the Black Knight in *Monty Python and the Holy Grail* who would not let King Arthur pass. First getting his arm cut off, where he said, "'Tis but a scratch, I've had worse." They continue fighting and his other arm is cut off, and he says, "Oh, had enough, eh? It's just a flesh wound." Arthur then chops off his right leg, and the Black Knight yells, "I'm invisible... the Black Knight always triumphs! I will have you! Come on, then." After this second leg is cut off and he falls to the ground, he says "Oh? All right, we'll call it a draw."

Like the Black Knight, I took a lot of hits and often did not notice the damage it was doing to me, my family, and my relationships until it was too late.

LIVE Application

Learning to use the tools, resources, and armour available for DIE can you help weather the ups and downs of the work. It is important to understand how you can take care of yourself. Otherwise, if you are out of commission, you will not be able to take care of others.

You cannot use the position or armour as your identity. Police and other professionals are assumed to have **integrity**, but you need to practice and demonstrate your integrity on and off the job.

Sometimes **valour** can be seen be false bravado. Authentic courage in standing up for what is right will be noticed and appreciated by all.

The problem with armour is that it puts barriers between you and others. Look at the average police car, driving around with two clad centurions in its bubble. Are they approachable? Do they look like they want to have a heartfelt conversation with us? If we want to **engage** with others, we need to build bridges, not walls.

FOOD FOR THOUGHT:

1. What is your armour that protects you or that you are hiding behind?

2. Have you ever avoided calling someone out for their discriminatory actions because you were afraid of harming your relationship with them?

CHAPTER 9

WHAT CARD IS IN YOUR WALLET? – PLAYING THE RACE CARDS

ONE THING I HAD STRUGGLED with originally in DIE was owning and being proud of my identities, positions, and privileges. During my career in policing, I investigated many crimes involving people from a wide variety of backgrounds. I served all Calgarians in a consistent LIVE manner, irrespective of whether they were victims, witnesses, or suspects. I had the opportunity to be lead investigator in many high-profile cases and in some cases where the offenders were from immigrant backgrounds.

On one such case there was a group of Lebanese criminals who were terrorizing Calgarians with home invasion, robbery, assault, and intimidation. Through my investigation and with the support of confidential informants, I identified the ring leaders—a pair of Lebanese brothers. These juveniles were extremely smart and had a network of family and friends they called their "cousins" who they could call on at any time to do their bidding and intimidate all others from testifying against them or "ratting." Over a short period of time, I was able to get enough evidence to charge them, and with that their invisibility deteriorated, encouraging others to come forward. I arrested them several times, and on our last trip together driving to the police station, one of them blurted out, "Constable Stewart, the only reason that you are picking on us is because you are racist and don't like us Lebs." I have had many people challenge my integrity before, but for someone who was so guilty to pull out "the race card" was truly an offence. I pulled the car to the curb and turned around to look them both in the eye. I said very calmly and proudly, "I am Lebanese, and what you both have been doing is an embarrassment to your family, your heritage, and me." They were silent the rest of the trip to their cells. A few months later, they approached me after their final court case and thanked me for arresting them and putting them on a better path. They did not realize the harm they were doing had such a negative impact on their family and community. In following up on their progress, both brothers completed school, have been successful in their chosen professions, and are good citizens of Calgary.

I know that having certain physical cards, like my police badge, government credentials, and even a post-secondary diploma, has provided me with access to additional resources, as well as more positive treatment in certain situations. In retrospect, I have had to recall when I played my "race card" to get anything. Consciously, I did not realize that my Whiteness offered protection or access to certain privileges. Thinking back, I was surprised how readily accepted I was as I used my "Lebanese Card" when working with Middle Eastern communities.

It is important to remember that people from collective cultures, like Indigenous people or those who emigrated from the Middle East, South Asia, Africa, or Asian countries, value the importance of community and family over individual needs. Our Western criminal justice system is based on Judeo-Christian values, of individual punishment and atonement (guilt), where collective cultures use community values of family and honour (shame) to correct behaviour. I have seen firsthand how restorative justice principles have solved issues and healed the community. Restorative approaches include feedback from all parties directly involved, including the family and friends impacted by the issue.

LIVE Application

It is a valuable **learning** exercise to take the time to think about whether you come from a collective or individual culture. Then identify whether you think your preferred way of thinking and operating is from the same perspective. You may also note that this may change depending on whether it is in a work, community, or family setting.

Whatever background and "race card" you hold, you should use it with **integrity.** It can be a powerful tool, but if it is used willy-nilly, it will lose its value.

It can be a difficult and painful process to investigate how you have benefited from your culture, background, or appearance. It takes real bravery and **valour** to critically reflect upon yourself.

As you **engage** in DIE work, it will become apparent which "cards" you hold and which are held by your colleagues. Work with others who have different "cards" to bring a variety of perspectives to your work and practice.

FOOD FOR THOUGHT:

1. If you were on the receiving end of a racial slur or in danger because of your identity, how would you react?

2. Can you recall a time when something you learned as a young person about a specific community turned out to be very wrong? What caused that shift in knowledge?

CHAPTER 10

LEARN – EARN – RETURN: THE CYCLE OF DIEING

I WAS AT A MUSLIM EVENT and heard a quote by a community and philanthropic leader, Mike Shaikh, about service. Learn – Earn – Return, which resonated with me at the time, meaning School – Work – Volunteering. You go to school and learn your vocation, then earn a living at that work, and in your final days, you have time to return gifts or give back to community by volunteering.

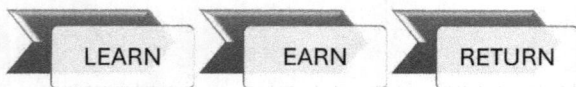

> LEARN   EARN   RETURN

I have always been a lifelong learner and believed I followed this path. I took lots of courses, police and academic, worked hard at providing for my family, and then began to volunteer more as I got older. Working with Indigenous communities, one lesson I learned was to think about and use holistic concepts. This included changing from linear models to circular. So, I applied and changed the Learn – Earn – Return to Learn – Unlearn – Earn – Return.

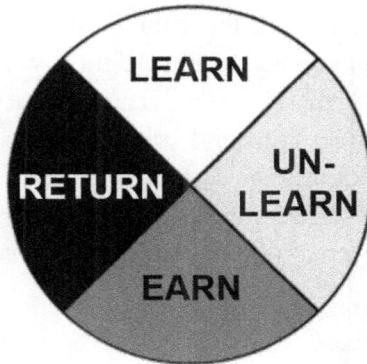

This translated to **learning** about investigating truths from a variety of sources, not just from Western and colonized thinkers. I needed to **unlearn** those lessons taught by Western thinkers and challenge the myths and stereotypes that have become part of my thinking. **Earning** is not about money and work; it's about earning the trust and respect from all those that I support and engage with. And then it is important for me to **return** these teachings to others. Unlike in linear thinking, in this circle we start and restart the process again and again.

When I was assigned to the police Middle East liaison position, I had very little knowledge of the Israeli or Jewish communities in Calgary. After meeting with many of the leaders of the synagogues, schools, and institutions, I was invited to participate in weekly Judaism lessons facilitated by Rabbi Menachem Matusof. From doing this, along with attending annual ceremonies and cultural events, I felt more relaxed in the community. I was also included in religious and family events such as bar mitzvahs and Menorah lightings, which helped me understand the personal effects hate crimes and incidents have on individuals and their community. At the same time, I spent time in the Muslim community, taking time to meet with wise Imams and community members and learn about the truths of Islam. This helped me build bridges between the Jewish and Muslim communities, which have historic mutual distrust and conflict around the world. At the same time, both these communities are targets of hate crimes and prejudices.

With the increase in hate and bias incidents in our community, I partnered with community leaders Derrick Shirley and Vilma Dawson to facilitate a full-day gathering we called the DiverCity Calgary Responding to Hate Crimes Forum. Fifty attendees from a wide variety of backgrounds produced several recommendations and tactical actions, including a Community Response Plan for the next time a hate occurrence happened. The plan was simple: All communities would come together with a common voice when hate happened against anyone, from any background. Up until that time, if there was a hate crime, only a member of the impacted community spoke up. Not long after the forum, a rash of antisemitic graffiti showed up at a Jewish cemetery and synagogue. With our response plan in hand, community partners jumped in and brought together more than five hundred people from all faiths to an event calling out hate in our city, with the refrain that hate would not be tolerated in our city and an attack against one of us is an attack against all. The mayor and chief of police attended and spoke at the "Say No to Hate" event. The offender was apprehended, and the event received extremely positive media coverage.

LIVE Application

As adults we must unlearn as much as we **learn**. We have had so much learning, programming, and experiences that have formed who we are, but these thoughts, ideas, and experiences also can bias our thinking and perspective. It is important to get a deep understanding of new concepts from a variety of sources, most importantly from local subject matter experts and those with lived experience. The unlearning process is often the most difficult, as many things are ingrained and validated over time. For me it was stereotypes about Indigenous people. I had to challenge my beliefs and then replace them with facts and stories from a non-Western point of view.

Being honest, especially with yourself, will provide **integrity** to your learning process. When you learn something that challenges your world view, you may be tempted to discard the new information or resist its messenger.

Valorous learners are often the most successful in their endeavours. They push themselves and others, challenge the status quo, and help change our society. This bravery can come at a cost, as many people will not be ready to confront their perspectives and may vilify your message and you.

Engaging with people is the best way to really know them. There is only so much you can learn from a book or a video. Interpersonal contact and communication with people will enhance and amply all other types of learning. This will also confirm or add nuance to the information you previously acquired. Last, once you have a relationship with a human source, you can go back to them for updated information, as the world and community change.

FOOD FOR THOUGHT:

1. How have you experienced a significant positive shift in your view of a racial group? Why did this happen?

2. DIE work involves making new connections and friends. How can you expand your social circle to include people from different backgrounds?

CHAPTER 11

DIE IS A TEAM SPORT – NEVER DIE ALONE

As an avid soccer fan and player for the police soccer team, I believed sports could bring cops and kids together. When I first started working with the Middle East community, I mentioned this to a Muslim leader, Nage Hage, and he thought it was a good idea. We put up a few posters to advertise a game on a local field. I was excited until we got to the field and only one youth showed up. My dreams were dashed, and I walked away like a dog with his tail between his legs.

A couple of years later, I reached out and formed the first Middle East Police Advisory Committee. This was an unprecedented group in the city. It included local community leaders whose backgrounds were from the countries in that region, as well as representatives from Muslim, Jewish, and Christian faiths. We had several meetings, and during one of them, I asked why their youth were not considering policing as a career. A Jewish leader, Richard Bronstein, piped up and said, "In our community you can only be three things – a lawyer, doctor, and a disappointment." Everyone laughed, and the Muslim representative Abdul Sourya replied, "Yes and you can add an engineer to that list!" That broke the ice, and as we laughed, we started to have some amazing conversations.

During a following meeting, I asked what all Middle East community members had in common and why they were in Canada. There was an overwhelming agreement that they came to Calgary for a better life for their families and children. As adults, they were willing to uproot themselves and their careers, with the hope of the "Canadian Dream" for their following generations. Most had multiple degrees, spoke several languages, and had well-paying jobs in their home country. They could weather the political, criminal, and military storms back home, but they knew it was not the best environment for their kids. I raised the idea of our committee hosting a football/soccer tournament for their youth. Everyone thought it was a wonderful idea, and within several months all the members were involved in planning, promoting, and producing the Diversity Cup Soccer Tournament. Six teams and about seventy youths were at the inaugural event. Over the next several years, the annual tournament grew, and over five hundred kids participated each summer.

One of the most effective ways I have learned to address difficult and complex problems is through working with others, collaboration, and using the process of collective action. This is when a group of people work together on a common problem. When doing this, it is important to always remember the phrase, "Nothing about us without us," meaning if the problem impacts a segment of the population, they need to be included in the process from the beginning. It is amazing sometimes how often this does not happen. I supported a "Homeless Charter" project being done by the Calgary Homeless Foundation. They had lawyers, police, and other advocates on the project committee, but no homeless people. I insisted that they should, so a Client Action Committee was formed, enlisting engagement of people with lived experiences of homelessness, and they were instrumental to the project's success.

Most groups, including workplaces, politics, service, and volunteer organizations, are still run by the Male, Pale, and Stale (MPS) segment of our society. Many MPS in leadership positions or middle management do not want to advance DIE strategies, and those who do are blazing trails alone. DIE work can be a lonely occupation, as you are often among the few people in your organization who take on this important role. Many of your managers, coworkers, colleagues, friends, and even family members may not fully understand or support your work.

That is where I was when I started my journey as a DIE practitioner in policing. I had a mandate, but no one in my organization could guide or support me. I was able to reach out locally at first to civilian people doing this work, and then nationally to other officers trying to navigate their way. I partnered with RCMP Sgt. Sam Anderson and Winnipeg Police Service Sgt. Ron Johanson to host a police diversity conference and start the Law Enforcement Aboriginal and Diversity (LEAD) Network. I didn't realize it at the time, but what we had built was a Community of Practice (CoP). A CoP is a group of kindred spirits who have similar goals and concerns, convening on a regular basis to help each other. The LEAD CoP was invaluable in helping me learn about the best practices and promising principles in the field, which I could bring into my practice. At the same time, I was able to mentor and help other existing or new practitioners support their individual and organizational goals. Being part of CoPs, connecting and meeting like-minded people, has helped me advance and celebrate successes of others, as well as support and console them when their initiatives do not proceed as hoped. My mentors and supporters in this work have been invaluable to my DIE journey and have included leaders in their fields, such as Anne-Marie Pham, Dr. Hieu Van Ngo, Dr. Darren Lund, Linda McKay-Panos, Dr. Valerie Pruegger, as well as Elders Doreen Spence, Cassie Eaglespeaker, and Dr. Reg Crowshoe. These individuals harbour an incredible amount of knowledge gained through academia, lived experience, and years of teaching others, and I have been honoured to have the privilege of being gifted some of their wisdom.

The use of CoPs has been a foundational part of my DIE journey. CoPs are an opportunity for like-minded people to connect, collaborate, and commiserate as they try to make a difference. As a funder at the Alberta Human Rights

Commission, we participated in starting the Network of Indigenous Funders in Alberta (NIFA) and the Calgary Anti-Racism Funders Group. Both these CoP collaborations helped individual practitioners, their philanthropic organizations, and the communities we served. When the Rotary Indigenous Relations Committee was formed, we realized there were way more Rotarians interested in this work than we could support on a committee, so we started an Indigenous Learning CoP. We hosted Indigenous knowledge workshops and provided monthly updates of learning and engagement opportunities available in the community. This is probably one of the largest CoPs I have supported, with over 130 members.

Collective vs. Individual efforts – In this work, it takes personal commitment, learning, and actions, but that would never be enough. Successfully accomplishing organizational change requires a combined effort of leaders, champions, middle managers, and frontline people with the groups and teams, as well as support and advice from marginalized leaders, knowledge keepers, navigators, and individuals.

In policing I learned that you were never alone, and that always offered a huge sense of support. If you were ever in immediate danger and needed assistance, a "Code 200" callout (officer in trouble) would have every car in the city backing you up in record speed. Conversely, we used to say to offenders who would try to get away, "You can outrun me, but you can't outrun the radio"—meaning my follow officers were just a call away. It takes a team to do anything worthwhile, and I know that DIE teammates are just a call away.

LIVE Application

Learning with and through others can take loneliness and isolation out of DIE work. Finding like-minded co-conspirators, collaborators, and convenors will advance your efforts in amazing ways. It will help you and others move forward in a more timely and effective way.

Integrity is when you go into a situation with an open mind and actively listen to others. Too often we have our preferred vision on how a project should go and tune out the diverse ideas and creativity that could make it better.

In practicing DIE, you should have the courage to face the dangers and challenges. This **valour** can be an internal struggle, as we challenge ourselves and our perceptions. Many times, our greatest growth and aha! moments happen when we see an alternative that is better than what we had originally imagined.

Engaging with as many diverse people as possible will advance your efforts. When hosting events for facilitating discussion, we must invite and include those with subject matter expertise and lived experience from different cultures, countries, religions, genders, sexual orientations, and ages. This is equally as important as when you would traditionally build a team or board by including people with a variety of backgrounds in education, experience, and skill sets.

FOOD FOR THOUGHT:

1. When have you been vulnerable with others by sharing your successes and failures?

2. A major skill required when you start to DIE is the ability to network with people who can collaborate with you or support your work in some way. How many people in your network come from a background that is different from yours?

3. For your next event, how will you bring together people from different cultures to work towards a common goal?

CHAPTER 12

YOUR NETWORK IS YOUR NET WORTH

Even though I came from humble beginnings, being raised by a single mother and only just barely completing a high school education, I still had the opportunity to succeed in our country. I worked hard to support my family, often doing two or three jobs, and always left people, places, and projects in a better place. I found myself on committees or around people who were above my perceived station in life. My voice seemed to matter in professional and political circles. In retrospect, I was welcomed into some of these circles because I looked like them or understood their worldview. I was gaining some privilege in society, which was in many ways due to the increasing number of people I considered to be my network. Working with and engaging with people from culturally diverse backgrounds, I followed the mantra of "Your network is your net worth," meaning your ability to authentically connect with people can advance your personal value to an organization's mandate. Net worth is often calculated on the financial value of the assets of a person or organization, and rarely on skills and abilities that lead to building positive relationships or outcomes. Networking has been proven to enhance success in DIE by building social capital as well as nurturing interpersonal and institutional relationships.

When I joined the Alberta Human Rights Commission, I already had a large range of contacts from various sectors (I had amassed quite a collection of business cards, contacts on a Rolodex, and names on my phone). This included people I had met who were from diverse backgrounds or represented corporate, nonprofit, and government organizations. But how could I leverage these relationships and knowledge to advance human rights and diversity in our province? I quickly realized that as a government representative, I was in a unique position to view this work from a three-thousand-foot view to empower and build capacity of marginalized people, while also advocating and impacting changes in organizations and systems. Many times, my networking abilities led to convening or being asked to sit at collaborative tables. My manager, Susan Coombes, was giving out gag gifts one Christmas and presented me with an extension cord. I was confused until she explained that I was great at "connecting" people together. In my funding role, I was able to connect those in need of funding with what grants were available, as well as identify opportunities, skills, and resources for funders and philanthropists to timely respond to community need.

Networking is invaluable in building collaborative relationships that lead to real change. It is the constant tool that underlies collective action and constellation-type initiatives. It is well documented that complex issues are best addressed by the collective efforts of many stakeholders. I have used existing networks and been invited into others to address difficult societal problems, such as gangs, human trafficking, homelessness, hate, and racism. After facilitating conversations about human rights concerns, I invited five communities (Fort McMurray, Edmonton, Red Deer, Calgary, and Lethbridge) to join the Coalitions Creating Equity (CEE). This initiative helped leaders in each of these locations build relationships and tools to address discrimination issues their communities were facing, using collaborative and cooperative efforts.

A DIE networker needs to be able to work with people from all backgrounds and walks of life, as well as have a firm understanding of the mandates and systems of many sectors, organizations, and work areas. In addition, the best networkers are those who can merge their connections to take advantage of direct and indirect contacts. The DIE networker or engagement specialist does not need to have all the answers but is the one who can find the most appropriate person who does. In meetings, I am often asked if I know a person who has a certain background or set of skills. Often, I can leverage my network and connect people appropriately, and you can too.

LIVE Application

To network, on behalf of your organization, the first thing you need to **learn** is why you and your organization value DIE and then translate that into a concise "elevator speech" that is tied to your purpose or mandate. You are confirming and communicating What's In It For ME (WIIFM). This is not about being self-centered; it's about being self-aware. Once you understand that, you can listen to those you meet, try to understand their WIIFM, and connect the dots to what goals and aspirations are in common.

Demonstrating **integrity** will encourage people to join your networks. This is about being a good example to others, sticking to your moral principles, and being transparent and open with everyone by telling and standing up for the truth.

> *Integrity is more valuable than income.*
> *Honour is richer than fame.*
> *Self-worth is wealthier than net worth.*
> —Robin Sharma

Valour in networking means getting out of your comfort zone. Try starting an honest conversation with someone you do not know. Too often, I have seen networking events where cliques are formed and where old acquaintances spend their time catching up. By being brave, you will expand your network and net worth.

When you **engage** with others, be present with your mind and soul. Embrace the conversations in the now, without daydreaming or thinking about where your next appointment is. This also means putting away your phone and laptop, which more than likely distract you from the people right in front of you.

You only have one chance to make a first impression. When you are working in DIE, take the time to do it right.

FOOD FOR THOUGHT:

1. In what ways do you have influence in a situation or are a privileged person compared to others?

2. How does your network give you additional advantages, power, or privileges?

CHAPTER 13

SUPERPOWERS – DIE POWER AND PRIVILEGE

MOST OF US, ES-PECIALLY THOSE living in Canada and the United States, have first world problems and, therefore, privileges others can only dream of. That is not to say that all privileges are equal or that all people in North America have equal opportunities to succeed. I know the fact that I am a Caucasian male of European descent, heterosexual, and with no visible disabilities does not limit my opportunities to work, live, or enjoy recreational activities in my city.

Statistically, I am less likely to be discriminated against and more likely to earn a higher income. Long before there were conversations of allyship, I took the time to listen to and learn about the experiences of marginalized populations in our country and confront prejudices when I saw them, as well as advance policies and programs that removed barriers caused by racism and discrimination.

Almost everyone remembers where they were during the attacks of the World Trade Center in New York on September 11, 2001. I was the Calgary Police Service's Middle East Liaison Officer, a position I'd held for two years. When it was learned that the attacks were committed by nineteen militants associated with the Islamic extremist group al-Qaeda, I knew, as the Middle East liaison officer, that there would be backlash towards Muslim people in the United States, but I did not anticipate how much hate and violence there was going to be in Canada and within our communities in Alberta. It was extremely disturbing to read the police files, see the reports in the media, and hear about the Islamophobic incidents in the community. Local Muslim leaders emphatically denounced the attacks, but that did not dissuade mainstream community fearmongering and attacks.

As a subject matter expert on the Muslim community, I was interviewed by several major news outlets. Using my position as a White police officer, I said, "Ninety-nine percent of Calgary's Muslim community members are God-fearing, hard-working Canadians who, like the rest of us, are here to make society better for their families and neighbours," and "We should not demonize our brothers and sisters for something they do not support and have nothing to do with." I was astonished to see that the power of my words helped de-escalate the fear and apprehension being felt by Calgarians. My comments, supported by others, helped educate and influence the thoughts and actions of the mainstream population.

While I was the board president of Calgary Learns, I noted that the organization funded few, if any, programs for Indigenous adult learners. The organization's mandate was to remove barriers and support foundational learning for adults. This was astonishing to me, as it was well known that Indigenous people have lower literacy levels and educational achievement than the general population. I mentioned this to Executive Director Krista Poole, who brought this up with staff members, where there were excuses and resistance. Reasons included that Indigenous people were already accessing mainstream programs, Indigenous groups were not applying for grants, and there were First Nation jurisdiction issues. I realized that I had influence and power as the president, so I worked with the executive director to prioritize Indigenous learner programs within our mandate.

To do this, the organization hosted circle dialogues with elders and community leaders to identify what the barriers were for Indigenous organizations and learners and to look at options to improve the situation. Calgary Learns worked with the community to create the first-of-its-kind Indigenous funding stream for literacy grants, including decolonizing its funding processes to include oral application and reporting processes as well as Indigenous reviewers. They have shared their journey with other funders and philanthropic organizations that have followed suit in changing their granting processes, which has improved access to not only Indigenous groups, but also to those that traditionally were underserved or excluded.

When I joined the Alberta government in 2008, very few of the Human Rights Education and Multiculturalism Fund's grants went to Indigenous-led projects. Although, there was an acknowledgment that Indigenous people were victims of an above-average amount of discrimination and racism. The year prior to joining the commission, I had published a hate crime report that identified Indigenous people as one of the most likely communities to be victims of hate crimes and incidents, while at the same time they were less likely to report them to authorities or access resources to address them. I worked hard with our team to change processes, and I used my position to increase our outreach and relationships with Indigenous leaders.

In one of the Spider-Man movies, Peter Parker says, "With great power comes great responsibility." Looking back, I am proud that I used my power as a White man and the power of the institutions I represented to make positive change. Each of us has some power in almost every situation, including with our family, community, study group, or workplace.

> *"Having power is not nearly as important as what you choose to do with it."*
> —Roald Dahl

LIVE Application

Take the time to **learn** what powers (and privileges) you have that can be used to support a person or group of people who do not have access to certain resources.

Consider how your education and credentials can open some doors or provide credibility to a project.

Be honest with yourself about what powers you have. Have the **integrity** to own your privileges, while looking for opportunities to use them to help someone less fortunate. "Nearly all men can stand adversity, but if you want to test a man's character, give him power"—Abraham Lincoln.

The truest test of **valour** is to dare to use the powers and privileges you were born with, as well as those that worked so hard for the good of humanity. It is easier to sit back and personally enjoy your privileges than it may be to share them with those who are less fortunate.

Just like Marvel or DC superheroes, you do not have to always use your superpowers. Learn and practice when to **engage** your superpowers in different situations. You can use them in private (when no one is looking) or in public (with colleagues, coworkers, and community).

Your superpowers will be to DIE for!

FOOD FOR THOUGHT:

1. Have you ever wondered if there is more you can do to make the world a better place with the power and privileges that you hold? And what did you do to make it happen?

2. What are some of the important life lessons you learned from your grandparents or aunts and uncles?

CHAPTER 14

WHO ARE YOU? DIEING WILL BE THE LAST THING YOU DO.

AT CERTAIN POINTS IN OUR lives, we ask ourselves, "How did I get here? Where I am going? And what am I leaving behind for those who follow me?" But what does this have to do with DIEing?

In *Alice's Adventures in Wonderland*, the Caterpillar asks Alice, "Who are YOU?" She replies, "I–I hardly know, sir, just at present—at least I know who I WAS when I got up this morning, but I think I must have been changed several times since then."

In our world we have multiple identities and can wear many hats. I have earned my living as a police officer, contractor, handyman, government employee, consultant, and entrepreneur. I am a husband/partner, father, grandfather, brother, uncle, son, and friend. Of all those, my favourite title is Grampa, and it is what keeps me doing DIE work. I strive to create environments where my grandchildren and all their peers have equal opportunities to succeed, no matter their gender, sexual orientation, the colour of their skin, and their ancestry.

As humans, we tend to spend a lot of our time thinking about the present or future. Much of what we are today is because of our surroundings and lineage. We all know the debate over nature versus nurture, but how often do we acknowledge and use that history to help us move forward in a positive way? Through my teachings with Indigenous elders and knowledge keepers, I learned the important lesson of bringing ancestors into my prayers and conversations. We are surrounded by the presence and spirit of all living things, as well as rocks, plants, bodies of water, and those who came before us. Often Indigenous people may finish a prayer or comment with the phrase, "All my relations." With the increase in ancestry sites and tests and people uncovering stories about their family's past, many are gaining a better understanding of where they come from and the strengths of their ancestors.

On my own path to self-discovery, it has been invaluable for me to learn what obstacles people overcame to make a better life for their descendants and what I can do for my grandchildren, as well as all those in our country. My Aziz family came to Canada early in the last century to escape Christian persecution from the Ottoman Empire. They had several businesses in the Toronto area and then tried homesteading in southern Saskatchewan. My mother, Delia, was born in a sod hut and raised on the farm before the family returned to Toronto, as her brothers were called to fight in the Second World War. My grandmother, Rose (Rohesia), was the matriarch of the family, raising the family and making money by tailoring for the neighbourhood. She lived to the ripe old age of 105. On the other side of my family tree, the Stewarts immigrated to Canada to escape the Great Famine of Ireland. They also tried to farmstead in the west and had a farm in Lacombe, Alberta (I still the have the cowbell from their favourite life-giving livestock, "Old Moll"). These were tough times as well, and the Stewart clan returned to southern Ontario and settled down in Hamilton. Often, I will ask one of my ancestors to join me in a meeting or in meditation. More than likely, I will call on my grandmother, Siti, as she helped raise me and was one of the most inspirational people I have known.

My friend, former police officer and Piikani Nation Councillor Cindy Provost, taught me a valuable tool to bring added wisdom into space. When starting some meetings, I ask the participants to invite an ancestor to join us when they introduce themselves and to share why they chose this person. Inevitably it will be someone who was a leader in their home and community and who has a connection to the topic in discussion on that day. I was asked to facilitate an inaugural meeting of a Rotary club's Indigenous Relations Committee, and I requested that attendees invite a member of their family. Six of the twelve disclosed that their invitee was Indigenous. Others revealed that their in-laws or grandchildren were of Indigenous heritage. This was a powerful moment for the group, as they were able to share an important part of their history and why this work matters with colleagues who had not felt safe to do previously. The room was electric, and you could feel the occupants double in the room from twelve to twenty-four.

LIVE Application

Many of our relatives have done the hard work of following their roots by researching ancestors and building family trees. This is an opportunity to **learn** about your ancestors and connect with them. There are many online resources to help you with this quest. Find out where your predecessors came from, what obstacles they overcame, and how you are similar or different.

When doing this research, it is important to be honest with yourself about what you learn. Have the **integrity** to uncover and understand the good and bad things about your family and forefathers. They were humans, like us, trying to navigate their turbulent times.

Have the **valour** and bravery to own your history and ancestry. We see a growth of diverse people celebrating their identities, and we should support them. At the same time, we should be available to boldly cherish and proudly honour our own.

Engage with your family and their stories. Take the time to reach out to your elders (dead or alive) and connect with them. Look at the old pictures, hear their stories, and ask questions. You will learn about yourself in the process and discover new opportunities for growth.

FOOD FOR THOUGHT:

1. Write down an ancestor, relative, or friend who passed away who you would like to join you on your journey to DIE. What special powers or inspiration do they bring? How and why do you feel in their presence?

2. Who do you hope to inspire in the next generation, and how would you want to be remembered?

3. You have probably experienced what it is like to accidentally offend someone because of the words you just said. Awkward and embarrassing, right? How would you change the interaction if you could have a "do-over?" Or how could you make it right?

CHAPTER 15

HOWDY, PARTNER! – THE LANGUAGE OF DIE

HAVE YOU EVER SAID THE wrong thing in a group setting or cringed when you heard someone else do that? Language matters, and its context changes over time and from community to community. It is important to do your homework and identify the most up-to-date and appropriate terms to use when you are working with diverse groups. While working in policing, I attended the Alberta Rockies Gay Rodeo Association annual rodeo with my coworker and friend Doug Jones. Doug was the police liaison officer for the 2SLGBTQ+ community and hate crimes, and I was the diversity training officer and Middle East liaison officer for the department. We were in plain clothes (not wearing our uniforms) and hosting a booth at the entrance to the event.

Doug was well known in the community, and he proceeded to introduce me to everyone as his "partner." After shaking hands with dozens of leaders, he suddenly changed the introduction to "colleague." As soon as he said that, I burst out laughing, realizing that a police partner has a much different connotation than the word "partner" has in the same-sex community, where it means a person who you have an intimate relation with. This scenario shows the importance of how to DIE laughing. This work can be tough and is seriously important, but you must find fun and humour in it at times if you want to do it for a long time. During the annual rodeo, we were encouraged to enter the competitions. We signed up for the goat dressing event. Once signed up for this camp event, we were goaded by the organizers continually. They said, "You are not going to let some gay beat you, are you?" I was shocked when I heard that, as I would never talk like that, but I realized that community members can use language that a White heterosexual male can't. At the same time, it occurred to me that we had gained their trust and were being allowed into the humour and language of the group. In the two-person goat dressing event, you run fifty feet to where a goat is tethered to the ground. One of the team members has a pair of jockey-style underwear that he wears over his forearms. The team member without the underwear picks up the goat's rear hooves, grabs the underwear from around the other member's arms, and pulls it up the legs of the goat. Both team members must then race back and cross the start/finish line to stop the time. The underwear must stay over the goat's tailbone until the timer is tagged by both members. We placed second two years in a row, so they got the last laugh!

One thing I learned over the years is that hearing one's name pronounced properly brings a smile and glow to that person. It has been said that there is nothing more beautiful than the sound of your own name. For most it brings a sense of joy and pride. My wife, Marina, gets particularly angry when someone mispronounces her name as "Maria," as she connects that with names maids are given on Telenovelas (Latin soap operas). When we were dating, Marina called me "Ken," and I never corrected her, as I thought it was due to her accent. It was only when all her family and friends also called me Ken and put it in writing that I figured I should set the matter straight. There is rarely a good excuse for mispronouncing someone's name, and it can be offensive if it is done more than once. A good practice to get into is to ask people the history of their name, what names or pronouns they preferred to be called by, and how to pronounce their first or last names. This can be a good icebreaker and conversation starter. It shows interest in the person and their community.

Working with many cultures, I have found that a good icebreaker is to know how to say in their language, "Hello, how are you? I am fine, thank you." It is a simple gesture that shows you are trying and have come prepared to build a relationship. Saying "Salam Alaikum" in Arabic, "Shalom" in Hebrew, "Namaste" in Hindi, "Bonjour" in French, "Buenos Dias" in Spanish, "Oki" in Blackfoot or "Tansi" in Cree are all important ways to start a conversation or give greetings at an event. I taught this technique to a group of senior police officers. One of them was trying to remember "Sut Shri a Cul"—"hello" in Punjabi—and he put it into a context that he would remember: "Sucks going to this call." We all laughed, and then about a month later he tracked me down and said it was an extremely useful technique. As a traffic officer, he had to notify a Sikh family about a serious injury their young daughter incurred in a car accident. As he went to the door, he greeted the family elder with "Sut Shri a Cul Gi" (Uncle). The man's stern and concerned face relaxed, and he invited the police into his home. The conversation went better than expected, and the officer felt that taking the time to learn and introduce himself in this culturally appropriate way helped him be more effective in his job.

A simple and inexpensive way to demonstrate your openness to other cultures and doing things differently is to have your business cards in the language of the community you are trying to engage with. For instance, when I was the Middle East liaison officer, the back of my card was in Arabic. I noticed whenever I presented my card with the Arabic side up, the person would do a double- or triple-take and often make a comment—anything from "That's cool" to "Where did you get that done?" to even "Who translated this for you? It's wrong." It was always a conversation starter that made people smile. While working in the areas of human rights and DIE, my cards were always translated and stamped in Braille. Only a few people from the visually impaired community received the card, but almost everyone who did felt the tactile bumps and took the time to appreciate it.

LIVE Application

Do research on a community and **learn** what terms and language are appropriate. For instance, using the term of Indigenous people versus First Nations, Métis, Inuit, Aboriginal, Native, Indian, etc. Understand the difference between people and their faith. For instance, are they

Muslim individuals who study Islam? Or are they Jewish people who follow Judaism?

Having **integrity** in language means not assuming that Western ways or the English language is better or preferred in other cultures. Contrary to the schoolyard rhyme, "Sticks and stones may break my bones, but names will never hurt me," words can and do have adverse impacts on people. It is important to use the best and most appropriate words that lead to building trust and positive relationships.

It takes bravery to step outside of your comfort zone and even challenge your own assumptions and the status quo. Be **valorous** in asking questions of those you meet. There is never a dumb or stupid question; each one is an inquiry into the unknown. People will appreciate your boldness, as well as your being a humble seeker of wisdom.

Engagement is about authenticity, respect, and openness. It is valuable to connect with people through language and see similarities as well as differences.

FOOD FOR THOUGHT:

1. When you embark on DIEing, you will quickly learn that using the right terms with people who are racialized or who are members of the 2SLGBTQ+ community is extremely important. Think of terms you may have used in the past, and which ones you use now—for example, "handicapped" versus "a person with a disability."

2. How have your family or friends impacted the way you see and interact with others? Reflect on the equity-seeking experiences of your own family and friends. What have you learned?

CHAPTER 16

LA FAMILIA – LIVING TO DIE

I AM SURE WE HAVE ALL had a feeling of being a fish out of water, out of our comfort zone or natural environment. That is how I often felt with my real-life version of TV's *Modern Family* sitcom, with me being the White, male, North American patriarch, and my wife being from Colombia, South America.

As I've mentioned, I come from a loving and large Lebanese family. Outside of the annual Aziz gatherings, I spent most of my young life with my sister, Lisa, in a nuclear family, and I saw similar arrangements among my friends. This meant that I was used to perceiving the "normal" family unit to be made up of a man and woman with a couple of children. When I got older and had kids of my own, I continued to follow this model. This all changed when I married Marina, from Colombia, and we blended our family and raised five kids together. I did not realize how big our clan would grow, as I learned that large, tight-knit families are important in her culture.

Even though her parents, siblings, nieces, and nephews were spread across the world, they were close and in constant contact with each other. We started supporting many of her family members to immigrate to Canada and to host others for their vacations. There is nothing more humorous, or embarrassing, than leaving or arriving at an airport with an entourage of a dozen or more people. I got used to it, but it never stopped putting a smile on my face. Our family was growing quickly, and it did not stop there. Marina was very involved in the Canadian Colombian community, starting several nonprofits and helping others settle in Calgary. Our family gatherings were starting to grow each year, and at times I felt like we were godparents in the community.

The incoming community members needed lots of support, and we did what we could. Among the many things Marina initiated, she founded a Colombian dance group, so the youth would be able to learn and experience their cultural traditions. The group did not have any money or a place to practice, so I arranged for them to use the police gym once a week. As they got better and bigger (there were over thirty of them), they needed traditional outfits, so we dug into our savings and purchased the necessities. The dance troupe performed in many venues, and the highlight was when Marina and her community partners entered them and a float into the Stampede Parade. It was a hit. It even had a donkey and coffee sacks with the iconic Juan Valdez character.

It was not until a few years later when the youth had grown into successful adults that we realized what an impact we'd had on their lives. Many of them stayed connected, shared their family and personal triumphs, and acknowledged how our acts of kindness and caring contributed to their integration into Canadian society. I have grown as a man since joining La Familia Pardo-Uribe and being welcomed into the homes of many Colombians, in Canada and abroad. Seeing newcomers struggle and overcome obstacles to make Canada their home has awakened my sense of country and patriotism.

Being bicultural, European, and Arabic, as well as embracing Latin culture, has empowered me to look at DIE in a different light. I often use the analogy of a buffet—I have been able to belly up to the food stations and try different delicacies. The ones I like I will add to my plate and even go back for seconds. This has worked better for me than relying on my traditional, passed-down ways of doing things. For instance, I have learned to be a better host for work or personal gatherings from being hosted by South Asian community members. After observing Indigenous grandparents support their families and children by taking on more active parental roles, I have welcomed the opportunities to do that for my kids and grandchildren. Most importantly, I have modified my individualistic and capitalistic ways over time by watching collective community approaches to work and life, leading to prioritization of family and relationships first. This has really helped me LIVE life large.

LIVE Application

It is enlightening to **learn** and explore the values of your own culture and background. Some of these you may wish to embrace, while others may not fit in with your life-style—and that is okay. With the diversity available now in our society, it is a great time to dive into other ways of being and thinking. In my learning journey over the past few years, I have done more investigations into my Arabic ancestors as well as Marina's Colombian roots.

Having **integrity** with family and relationships means developing and defending your inner and outer values. These values can change over time, but you must commit to honour, live, and communicate them.

Change is hard work, especially when your family or organization has held strong cultural, political, or social attitudes for a long time. **Valour** and bravery are needed to challenge long-held beliefs, both yours and those of others, as well as incorporate new cultures and beliefs into your life and organization.

Engaging with family and community takes a commitment to genuinely make efforts to understand each other's beliefs, values, and priorities. This means taking the time to directly and indirectly connect with people. This may start out as seeing what you have in common, as well as what differences there are. More often than not, our similarities help to bridge the divisions that cause conflict and anxiety between people.

FOOD FOR THOUGHT:

1. Sometimes we do not fully understand what people from other cultures and countries have experienced until we have a similar experience ourselves. Think about your friends from different cultures and how they are integrating into our society. What can you do to help this process?

2. Have you ever been in a different country where you had an experience that opened your eyes to understand the challenges the people there face? How did you feel, and what helped you acclimatize better?

CHAPTER 17

ISLAND LIFE – YOU OKAY?

After retiring from the Calgary Police Service, I was invited to work for the Royal Cayman Island Police Service. I was hired because of my experience working with diverse cultures, and I became an officer skills instructor because I understood the criminal justice system (like Canada, it was based on British criminal and common law principles). This was an amazing opportunity to live and work in a culture where I, as a White person, was in the minority and had less privilege. In addition, as I was employed as an ex-pat on contract with temporary foreign work status, I had to learn what it was like to live in a foreign land with vulnerable income security. Luckily, I made several friends from around the world, like Raul Espinosa, who were going through the same scenario and provided guidance through my stay. I have fond memories of colleagues and community members greeting me as "Mister Cam." Rather than following that up with "How are you?" they say, "Are you okay?" This question always set me back, as I wanted to reply, "Why, is something wrong with me?" and had to actually think if I was truly okay.

Within three months of arriving, the island was hit by a once-in-a-hundred-year hurricane named Ivan. It decimated the small island community, and everything was in turmoil. Like most natural disasters, it impacted everyone indiscriminately. Rich or poor, Black or White, resident or non-resident, all were left without a dry home, electricity, or food. Marina and I lined up in food lines, lived in shelters, couch-surfed, and relied on the generosity of strangers. When I was in uniform policing a food line, I was approached by an older White gentleman who asked how I was doing and where I was living. Learning that I was without a home, he asked if I could house-sit his residence on the beach while it was getting fixed and he was off the island. I jumped at the chance to have a roof over our heads, but I realized later that he only offered me this opportunity because of my race and occupation. Once we found a place to safely live, we wanted to give back as well.

On the Cayman Islands, there were only about thirty-five thousand Caymanian residents and about the same number of expats. With such a small population, many of them were related and everyone knew everyone. A common greeting for the local Caymanians was "Who ya fah (for)?" meaning, "Who are you? Who are your parents, siblings, grandparents, and extended relatives?" I found this was like living in rural Canada or on First Nations reserves. This came up often in policing: When you arrested or questioned someone, they were inevitably related to the senior police or elected officials. On one occasion, after I pulled over a drunk driver, he handed me his cell phone. I put my ear to the receiver and, to my surprise, the chief of police introduced himself and asked what was happening. He asked me what the situation was, and much to the chagrin of the driver, the chief did not get involved in my investigation.

The Cayman Islands, like a lot of islands in the Caribbean, was colonized by Europeans who had slaves of African ancestry. Most Caymanians can trace their roots back to the slaves and the 116 families who owned them when slavery was abolished in 1833. Many of the residents looked down on the temporary residents, particularly those like me from North America or Europe who were employed in their financial, tourism, and service industries under work permits. The nepotism and discrimination raised its ugly head one day when I went to a police inspector's house to arrest his son for an assault. The inspector's wife came to the door and immediately began to say that this was her people's island, and that I was not welcome. She went on to say, "Ivan should have taken you and all your White people out to the ocean!" I was stunned and did not rebut or challenge her diatribe. I knew she had the power, connections, and influence to pull my work permit and send us back to the Great White North. Well, if I wanted to know what it felt like to be the victim of stereotyping and discrimination, I could not have had a more impactful lesson.

On that day, Mister Cam was *not* okay.

I continued to live and work on Cayman for about a year after Hurricane Ivan. I took on many roles for the police agency, including evaluating its arrest processes and training standards. I conducted in-depth evaluations and provided senior management with comprehensive recommendation reports. I was asked to submit all these reports with major changes to make the officers in charge look better. In some instances, the leaders responded that they had been operating with certain processes and procedures for hundreds of years, and who was I to tell them to change?

The problem was that the community and its justice system were in the twenty-first century, while the department was not. Criminal cases were being lost in court because of inappropriate handling of suspects and evidence. Even worse, officers' lives were being put at risk due to lack of training, inadequate equipment, and outdated policies and procedures. I could not in good conscience change any of my recommendations, and so I submitted my report to the powers that be as as-is. When they accepted my report but did not implement any changes, I made the decision to leave the service. About one month later, they said they would proceed with my recommendations and asked if I would return. I had to decline the offer for two big reasons:

I knew that organizational change with this department was going to be an uphill battle.

My family was growing with the birth of my first grand-child, Izzy, and I did not want to miss any time with her or my future grandkids. I realize that I was in a unique position, that I could leave the island and try to get back into my life in Canada, which was not the case for most of the residents there. Many Caymanians and other expats working on the island did not have the option of leaving, due to their financial or employment situation.

LIVE Application

It is a valuable lesson to try to **learn** what it is like to be in someone else's situation. Experiencing the challenges of being different allows you to have true empathy for those who experience discrimination and racism on a regular basis. In the Cayman Islands, I understand that many people see me as part of the colonial system that their ancestors lived through and that they may be still struggling with generational trauma today.

As you work with others and live with yourself, **integrity** is what makes you…you. Are you content when you look in the mirror at the end of the day? On the island, when I submitted the report on police training and processes, I knew that it was the right thing to do and may save an officer's life someday.

To "walk a mile in the other's shoes," you need to be brave. This **valour** may not be easy and can be very uncomfortable, but growth happens in those moments and experiences.

Engaging and connecting with other people expands one's views of themselves and the world around them. The more I entered the world of island life, the more comfortable I was interacting with community members on and off the job. This was really important on a small island, as not a day went by that I would not bump into someone I knew, whether it was in the grocery store or on the beach.

FOOD FOR THOUGHT:

1. Discrimination can happen to anyone. When have you or someone close to you been impacted by bias or discrimination?

2. Have you ever felt like you were a "fish out of water"? How might you help another person feel welcomed or get acclimatized to your workplace or community?

3. Have you ever been temporarily disabled because of an injury or other factor? Did it help you become more empathetic towards people who have a physical or mental disability all the time?

CHAPTER 18

CONCUSSIONS AREN'T REAL.
IT'S ALL IN YOUR HEAD.

H OW DO YOU FEEL RIGHT now? Better or worse than yesterday? As the army recruiting slogan goes, are you the "best you can be"? Besides having to wear progressive eyeglasses (newfangled bifocals), I consider myself able-bodied with some episodic disabilities like strains, sprains, and pains. I eat well, work out regularly, and I practice prayer and meditation.

As a Type A personality, I always push myself and my body to its limits. A few years ago, I overbooked myself into a fourteen-hour day, including multiple meetings and a three-hour drive to Edmonton. I checked in at about 10:00 p.m. and went to my room. As I was unpacking and getting ready to wind down, I walked by the corner of the bed, clipped it with my leg, and did the best flying header of my life, right into the wall. I looked at the dent in the drywall, staggered into bed with a massive headache, and decided I was in no mood for late-night television.

The next morning, to my astonishment, my headache was still there. I have had my share of hits to the noggin, playing soccer, being tall where there were small openings, and just being a bit of a klutz sometimes. Up until that day, I never took any pain medication for headaches, but this was different. So, on my way to an all-day meeting, I stopped by a pharmacy, grabbed some extra-strength Advil, and assumed everything would work out. Halfway through the day, I had to excuse myself due to the pain, and I drove with white knuckles back to Calgary. Once home, I crashed into my bed and woke up the next day feeling worse.

I went to the doctor, where I was told I had a traumatic brain injury, commonly called a concussion. Researching concussions, I learned that the symptoms can last from several days to weeks or longer. I have had lots of broken bones and injuries, and I have always been quick to recover. So, every day I would roll out of bed and have positive thoughts about my progress, only for my hopes to be dashed. I could not walk, drive a bike or car, work, or read. Worst of all, I could not play with my grandkids. It was not just physical; I was also feeling increasingly anxious and depressed. I thought "Is this the best I am going to be? And will this be my new normal?"

After a couple of months, I was willing to try anything, so I went to vision and physical therapies, which provided limited relief. I talked to my health providers and worked out a gradual plan to return to work. It was so gradual that it was frustrating, but every time I tried to push my limits, they pushed back, and I had to start again. I remember when I went to the office for the first time, I drove into the parking lot, had to sit for an hour to recover, and then drove home without getting out. This was going to be a tough journey. Luckily, I had great support from my family, work, and coworkers, as well as compassionate colleagues in the community. I would attend meetings, feel safe to disclose what I was going through, and ask for their understanding if I had to leave to address my symptoms.

The problem with having a traumatic brain injury is that no one knows what you are going through, including your doctors, friends, and family. There is nothing physical that can be seen, like a broken bone, cut, or infection. But this invisible disability was extremely painful and took a psychological toll. I have a real insight now into the life of many people with disabilities, and I hope this helps me to be a better advocate for their issues. I had taken my able body status for granted and felt trapped in my body and home.

It took me almost a year to be able to work again full-time, but to this day I still struggle with lack of concentration, irritability, sensitivity to light and noise, not getting enough sleep, depression, and anxiety. Some of this may be just age-related, and I understand that I need to listen to my body and only do what I have the capacity to do. This causes me some frustration, as I know what I could do before and often think I can be at that level again. As

George Burns said, "You can't help getting older, but you don't have to get old."

After having a disability, I realized that able-bodied citizens need to do more to remove barriers that impede people with disabilities (almost a quarter of our population) from fully participating in society. Most provinces in Canada, except for my province of Alberta and Prince Edward Island, have accessibility legislation. I teamed up with a group of disability self-advocates and allies to create Barrier-Free Alberta to fight for a provincial accessibility act that will proactively address physical barriers people may face. This would include ensuring that all new public facilities are built and services are provided using a universal design. Universal design is a concept in which products and environments are designed to be usable by all people, to the greatest extent possible, without the need for adaptation or specialized design.

I used the concept of universal design when the Alberta Human Rights Act was changed to include gender identity and gender expression as a protected ground. I noted that our building only had male or female bathrooms and no facilities for people who identified as transgender. I worked with our building management to find a space where we could convert a bathroom to "all gender." Once we found the location, we were able to add a changing table to it and ensure it was large enough for a wheelchair. Once completed, it was the most-used bathroom in the building, as it was accessible to all, including transgender, women with children, and people with disabilities.

Construction Cam

Like many police officers and firemen, I used my days off between shifts to build and renovate homes of family and friends. I continued to improve my handyman skills while working with people with disabilities and noted that it was very difficult for them to get into affordable accessible accommodation and often cost prohibited to renovate existing structures. When I retired from the commission, I joined Accessible Housing Calgary team as a contractor to transform existing bathrooms into safe and accessible spaces. It has been a true joy to see seniors with mobility issues and people with disabilities being able to stay in their homes for years to come. I am so blessed that I am able to combine two of my passions, construction and DIE for a positive impact in community.

LIVE Application

Learning about people with disabilities and how to create accessible communities is mandatory for our society to thrive in this generation. Expanding our collective and individual knowledge of visible and invisible disabilities will benefit everyone at some point in their life.

Doing this work, one must have an ethical and principled approach to supporting vulnerable and marginalized people. Having the **integrity** to be nonjudgmental and empathetic to the plight or condition of our fellow citizens

CHAPTER 19

POLITICS, PREJUDICE, AND POLARIZATION

H OW DO YOU GIVE BACK? For me, it has always been at the grassroots level, be it volunteering as a soccer coach for my kids' teams or sitting on committees. There is always a lot of "small-p" politics for us to navigate within organizations and groups, and I was naive in many ways to the larger games of politics in our society.

After living, working, and volunteering in the northeast and southeast communities of Calgary for several decades, I noticed that while this area was the most socially, ethnically, and economically diverse in the city, the people there were also the least likely to vote or be involved in politics. This started to trouble me, as a larger portion of this population was more likely to need services provided by government agencies but had little input in these programs. Many of the politicians in these areas were absent and not effectively engaging with their constituents from marginalized communities.

I worked for several political campaigns, including mayoral candidates Wayne Stewart and Naheed Nenshi, helping them outreach to diverse communities. Calgary, like most of Alberta, consistently voted for Conservatives in provincial and federal elections, and there was little hope of Liberals or other parties breaking that trend. I was rarely interested in politics, but I always kept up with current events, and I religiously voted. In 2010, the government of Canada, under the Conservatives, began changing our immigration and social policies in ways that were detrimental to Indigenous people, newcomers, and 2SLGBTQ+ communities. I could not stand idly by in good conscience. As Dr. Martin Luther King Jr. said, "A man dies when he refuses to stand up for that which is right. A man dies when he refuses to stand up for justice. A man dies when he refuses to take a stand for that which is true." So, I joined the Liberal Party of Canada, and with the support of my family and friends, I was a member of Parliament candidate in the 2011 and 2015 federal elections. My supporters included my wife, Marina, our daughters Connie and Jessica, my sister Lisa, Mother Delia, Mother-in-law Teresa, my grandson Kingston and nephew Simon. We had the most diverse team of volunteers in the city, and they devoted an amazing amount of time and talent. Many of them I now consider lifelong friends, like Mohammed Abouzeid, Steve Armstrong, Raghbir Basati, Camilo Gil, Perry Kavanagh, Avinash Khangura, Michelle Robinson, and Gerard Sinan. Like me, most of them had no experience in political campaigns, but they were passionate and willing to learn. Our events were electric, filled with joy and hope.

People on the east side of Calgary did not have the financial means or experience of donating to political campaigns, so our coffers were often bare. But we made do. Thanksgiving Day was celebrated during the middle of the 2015 campaign, and we could not take the time to have our traditional family get together. So, Marina and our family decided we should host a dinner at our campaign office. She cooked a turkey with all the fixings, and we invited all our volunteers and friends. I came to the office after a long day of door-knocking and found over one hundred people gathered there. Like the story of Hanukkah and the oil lasting for eight days, or that of Jesus feeding a multitude of people with five loaves of bread and two fishes, everyone feasted and celebrated the holiday together that night.

Having worked in DIE for over ten years at this point, I knew that there was a lot of politics within and between diverse communities. There is an immense amount of competition in these communities, as there are an infinite number of social issues, combined with a growing number of equity-seeking groups and subgroups. As a leader in the 2SLGBTQ+ community once told me, they and others are in the "Oppression Olympics." This became obvious during the campaign, with the numerous requests to meet with community leaders to hear and support their worthwhile causes. My heart ached for the group and individual challenges that were presented to me, particularly knowing that many of their requests might later fall on deaf ears.

We learned that politics was not all fun and games, as there was a lot of hatred towards Liberals and their progressive ideology, and towards immigrants who were allowed to enter Canada under previous governments. My family, including my daughters and grandkids, were harassed and threatened, and some volunteers were chased out of neighbourhoods. At one point we had to call in the police when our campaign office was surrounded by Conservative supporters banging their signs against the windows and chanting threats.

I was surprised to learn that politics and prejudice are intricately linked in our country. There was underlying and open xenophobia, which is the strong fear or hatred of foreigners and a dislike of people from other cultures or religions. As a person supporting people from progressive immigration policies and social programs, I was targeted in person and on social media. As the campaigns became more polarized, I became paralyzed and afraid to post any comments or statements of my own, as I was chastised several times by the party puppeteers.

We lost both elections to slim majorities. I gained immense respect for anyone entering politics, but I would not do it again, as it took a toll on me mentally, physically, and financially. During this process, I learned who my faithful friends were, and I gained many more. Shortly after the last election, my daughter Jessica said to me, "We are sorry for you that it was not the outcome you had hoped for, but we are happy that we have you back." It was a tough decision to enter the political arena and in some ways a tougher one to leave it, as so many people were behind me. I don't regret trying to make a difference in politics, as you only LIVE once.

After my run in politics, I used my relationships and connections in the Calgary's east side to make change. I joined and chaired Twelve Community Safety Initiative (12CSI) where we created a strategic vision and plan, hired its first executive director, Larry Leach, and developed safety and engagement programs that included ethnocultural and Indigenous perspectives. The organization created long-lasting partners with public safety and community organizations and has been recognized as a leader in crime prevention.

LIVE Application

You never stop **learning,** and sometimes, as they say, "Necessity is the mother of invention." Real growth happens when you learn something and apply it right away. I discovered more about politics of our nation and how to be a candidate in these two campaigns than I would have ever learned in a post-secondary program. Unlike school teachings, I will never forget these lessons or the people who were involved.

Political and personal **integrity** means exercising power consistently in the public interest and not using it to maintain your own wealth and position. It is about being ethical and using a principled approach when the cultural values of others conflict with yours.

Bravery and **valour** are not just for the battlefield of war but also for combating day-to-day issues like DIE. When entering these arenas, you may be stepping into treacherous environments and have limited hope of success. But that does not mean you should not go down that path or pursue a lost cause. In the movie *The Untouchables*, Malone, played by Sean Connery, holds his necklace as he tells Elliot Ness that it is a Saint Jude medallion, and that Saint Jude is "the patron saint of lost causes and policemen."

Civic **engagement** is the bedrock of democracy. We can only change our policy, programs, and politics by encouraging participation from all our citizens.

FOOD FOR THOUGHT:

1. Are you ready to DIE in public and stand behind your principles, at work, home, and community? What baby steps can you take now that will lead to your inclusive destination?

2. Do you think now is the time for change? Or are you going to procrastinate and wait until it is convenient or leave it for our children and the next generation to deal with?

CHAPTER 20

PEOPLE OF ACTION – DO OR DIE

I JOINED ROTARY IN 2011 AND left in 2016, as it did not meet my values and priorities at the time. In 2020, my friend and incoming Rotary district governor, Christine Rendell, invited me for a coffee. She is a strong supporter of diversity and inclusion and wanted to make some changes in the service organization during her tenure as its leader. I knew that as a female leader in business and the community, she had seen lots of exclusion and wanted to champion change for the organization. I agreed to invite and host a meeting of thirty people from diverse communities to discuss their perceptions of North American-based service organizations, such as Rotary. We heard there were many barriers to participating in traditional service clubs, including that they were not welcoming and not diverse organizations. People also said there were many service projects they would like to support if given the opportunity and the invitation.

Ten of the thirty attendees decided they wanted to continue the discussion about forming a unique Rotary club for and by people from diverse and immigrant backgrounds. They were very keen to get going. However, one month after starting the Mosaic Rotary Club of Calgary, COVID arrived in our city, and we were unable to meet in person for over a year. This was not ideal for a fledgling group with aspirations to build and grow a different kind of service space.

As the Mosaic Club was faltering, Christine asked me to join and chair the district's Diversity, Equity and Inclusion (DEI) committee. I declined the opportunity, but when asked to chair its newly formed Indigenous Relations Committee, I saw a chance to support an organization that was now ready for some change. Rotary District 5360 consists of over forty clubs and has about 1,500 members, called Rotarians. These clubs are in Southern Alberta, within the traditional territories of Treaty 7, which includes the Blackfoot Confederacy (Siksika, Kainai, Piikani, Stoney Nakoda Nations), the Chiniki, Bearspaw, Goodstoney, and Tsuut'ina Nations, and the Métis Nation within Alberta Districts 5 and 6.

I stepped into this role thinking there was a lot of support within the clubs and members and hoping there were many projects already moving forward. There were a few shining examples of projects that were making a difference, but these needed to be highlighted, amplified, and replicated across the region. What I learned was that some members were quite resistant to change and reconciliation efforts. In many cases, these people, who were long-standing members and leaders in their clubs, were preventing others from advancing Indigenous issues.

Once I stepped into the chair position, I found out that it was only a subcommittee of the DEI committee. I identified that it needed to be its own committee, with a budget and representation from the leadership team. I worked with the founding members and developed guiding principles for how we will work as a team, using both Indigenous and Western frameworks. The committee's founding Rotary members included Jim Bennett, Michael Bopp, Steve Leavitt, Chrisine Rendell, Brad Sewell, and David Wartman. A part of the ideology of this committee was that it would aim to have 50 percent representation from Indigenous non-Rotarians who would be paid a small honorarium for their service. Indigenous wisdom and input was provided by Elder Cassie Eagle Speaker, Tim Fox, Lorelie Higgins, Brad Spence, and Sandra Sutter. Honorariums are a traditional and long-standing practice when working with Indigenous communities. However, this was not a standard operating procedure for this and other nonprofit service organizations. I developed an honorarium policy for the district and had meetings with Rotary leaders where there was plenty of pushback. I said these items were non-negotiable if they want to do it right and have me involved. They agreed!

With the advice of our Indigenous members and elders, we identified that there needed to be three pillars for our strategy:

1. Building Rotarians' knowledge of Indigenous issues,

2. Informing Indigenous communities about Rotary,

3. Looking for opportunities to connect Rotarians with Indigenous communities.

One of our elders, Cassie Eagle Speaker, taught us to take our time and do things right, as "Relationships are built at the speed of trust." With his support, we made sure to integrate Indigenous ways of thinking and doing in our processes. This included consecrating (blessing) the strategy in a traditional pipe ceremony and coming to consensus using circle dialogues.

In addition to a small amount of core funding, the committee was awarded money from a district grant fund to support a project to help Rotarians and Indigenous communities members learn about each other through deliberate dialogues and facilitated engagement opportunities. Over the next two years, dozens of training sessions were hosted in the community, and several gatherings were hosted by the committee members. In addition, a Community of Practice (CoP) was started to support Rotary club champions and interested members, which grew to over 150 practitioners.

The committee asked Ina Fairbanks, a young Blackfoot artist, to develop a logo to promote our work. She was inspired by her teachings to include a graphic of two hands shaking on a mutual level, signifying building trust and friendship, within a traditional medicine wheel, representing our commitment to look at our work through an Indigenous lens.

This image resonated with our committee and the medicine wheel teachings I had received from elders. As a White man who is still learning Indigenous ways from elders and knowledge keepers, I have been told that when we look at the wheel, we always start facing east, where the sun rises and there are new beginnings. Its totem animal is the eagle, which has great eyesight and seeks the *truth*. The eagle and all its parts are a powerful symbol in the community. Then the south is the direction of the full warmth of the sun. The totem animal is a mouse, which knows intuitively those things that are *fair*. They are small but smart, and they know what is right. This is the place of building healthy relationships within families and communities. The blue section is the west, a place of spiritual striving. The totem animal is the bear, which uses introspection and its senses to build relationships and *goodwill*. Think of a warm bear hug. The north colour, white, symbolizes snow and the wisdom of the elders. The totem animal is the buffalo, which provides freely all that it possesses to the

benefit of the entire community. Buffaloes are wise, collective animals that look after their herds. In death, every part has a purpose for the tribe.

After being gifted this medicine wheel image with its four directions, I woke up with a jolt one night and realized there was a connection with Rotary—its four-way test guiding rules in what they say or do.

- Is it the **truth**? What are my understandings, perceptions, and experiences of Indigenous people?
- Is it **fair** to all concerned? Are my actions and those of my club equitably including Indigenous people?
- Will it build **goodwill** and better friendships? Am I inviting Indigenous people and those who are not from my background as friends?
- Will it be **beneficial** to all? Are our projects or investments benefiting Indigenous peoples?

For us to move forward and work together in the district, it was important for both Rotarians and Indigenous peoples to see themselves and their identities in the logo design.

I mentioned pushback, and there was plenty. Some clubs had heated arguments about land acknowledgments during their meetings. Individuals indicated that Indigenous issues were political in nature and therefore should not be part of Rotary meetings. Some of those people even resigned. We should be prepared to take a stance on our commitment to DIE, even if it means leaving an organization.

On the flip side, I heard from many more Rotarians who, like me, were looking for opportunities to support Indigenous people and projects. As it turned out, there were more people wanting to advance Indigenous work than resist it. I decided it was better to use my time and energy to work with those who wanted positive change rather than try to persuade, rebut, or change the minds of those fighting it. We learned it was important to provide support to champions within their clubs and ask others to give them space and not block their efforts.

One of the things I learned doing this work is that in every classroom, boardroom, or living room, there are people who are early adopters (one-third), fence-sitters (one-third), and resistors (one-third) on issues. If we can bring the fence-sitters (mushy middle) to join the people who are already committed to inclusion and reconciliation, then the two-thirds will be the majority of the group. It is important to help the majority be active in this work, rather than the usual silent majority we often hear of.

> *"If you want to bring a fundamental change*
> *in people's belief and behavior*
> *...you need to create a community around them,*
> *where those new beliefs can be practiced*
> *and expressed and nurtured."*

—Malcolm Gladwell, *The Tipping Point: How Little Things Can Make a Big Difference.*

The Unexpected Award

In December 2022, I learned that I had been nominated for and had become the recipient of the Rotary International Person of Action—Champion of Inclusion Award, for my work on this committee. I was shocked to learn that I was going to be one of six people in the world to receive this honour, which would be presented in Cape Town, South Africa, in 2023. I was conflicted, as we had made the efforts and been working as a collective, and this was an individual award. So, I reached out to our committee elders, knowledge keepers, and Indigenous and non-Indigenous members and asked for their advice. They all felt I deserved the recognition and the award would advance our collective work.

Western-based organizations like to highlight and acknowledge individuals and individual efforts as successes in society. The problem with that model is we know that teams made up of colleagues, collaborators, and cooperators are much more likely to produce the best results.

Champ vs. Chump – Did I deserve the award? How can I take credit for something we all should be doing? Sure, I was leading the initiative and pushing against some tides, but so were so many others in the trenches. How could

I leverage the award to create awareness and encourage others to take more action? If I did not accept it, would our endeavours be ignored or not have the impact we hoped for?

It was only after I decided to accept the award on behalf of the committee that I found out how big a deal this was in the "Rotary world." I got a chance to virtually meet the five other award winners, and they are true champions of inclusion from around the world, including İclal Kardıçalı from Turkey, who is helping Kurdish, Syrian, and Roma women and children through music; Rosemary Nambooze from Uganda, where she is an advocate for children with disabilities and for inclusive education; Sarita Shukla from India, where she supports the transgender community; Anderson Zerwes from Brazil, an advocate for 2SLGBTQ+, racial, and gender equality and disability rights; and André Hadley Marria from the United States, where she is the founding mentor of a program for entrepreneurs from underserved communities. I was the lone Caucasian, straight male in the bunch, and I was not sure my accomplishments or the committee's progress was deserving of this award.

Rotary, I learned, is one of the largest service organizations globally, with over 1.5 million members and 36,000 clubs in 200 countries, and as one leader pointed out to me, most of them are "male, pale and stale" (I identify as being from the first two of these). The Rotary International president for that year, Jennifer Jones, made diversity and inclusion a priority in her tenure. This would be the first and last of this award for Rotary, as they change the "Person of Action" category every year. It was going to partner with the Desmond and Leha Tutu Legacy Foundation to host a gala event for the awards in Cape Town, which would be televised internationally. Now I started getting nervous!

Getting Prepped for the Most Visible Role of My Life

Public speaking was not new to me. I have given workshops, provided greetings, been a keynote speaker, and presented to hundreds of audiences around the country and the world. I realized very quickly that this was going to be a different kind of animal when they let me know that Rotary had hired a professional presentation coach to support the "Champions of Inclusion" recipients. I spent many hours over a couple of months preparing and practicing delivering a five-minute "TED Talk" presentation before a live televised audience. The weight was enormous, as I had to represent not only myself but the collective efforts of so many back home in Canada.

First, I was advised to write my speech with fewer than seven hundred words. While writing it, I asked and received permission from elders and Rotarians to use their stories and quotes. How could I capture the journeys and successes of hundreds of people and at the same time inspire others to join the mission of advancing Indigenous people in such a limited number of words? I could not, so like a director doing a film, we worked at editing and left much on the cutting-room floor. After that, I was told to memorize and practice the speech exactly. This has not been my style of giving presentations, as I am more a shoot-from-the-hip-and-heart kind of speaker.

The process caused me more anxiety than you could know, but I persisted. There were several practice sessions with an audience and then a final one during the dress rehearsal.

During this last one, I also listened to the other presenters and did not hear the master of ceremonies acknowledge the Khoisan people, who were the Indigenous people of the Cape Town region. I asked the director if I could add one at the beginning of my talk, and he told me the show was on a tight schedule and could not fit this in. I said it was important to me, my teachings, and my elders, and that I would take the minute out of my time, if needed. The other award winners also felt it was important and were willing to give up some of their time as well. The director finally agreed, but there was no time to rehearse it.

On April 4, 2023, after walking on a red carpet into the historic theatre, I stood on the stage in front of cameras, lights, and over 250 people, including my mom and my wife, Marina. I started by thanking the land and its ancestral caretakers. To my pleasant surprise, the audience gave an ovation. This was a good start to what would be one of the best talks of my life.

Being in South Africa, where Apartheid had polarized and damaged the country for so many years followed by many years of reconciliation, was truly humbling. Meeting family members of Desmond Tutu, attending museums, and seeing the cell where Nelson Mandela was imprisoned for so many years helped me understand the magnitude of the issues that had happened half a world away from my home country. I realized that anything is possible through the hard work and dedication of a man or woman, no matter what their station is in life.

The gala event closed with a presentation of a beautiful custom glass trophy to the six of us and a standing ovation from the audience. I took the traditional pictures with the trophy, carted it back to Canada, and then put it on a shelf. It was shared with the District Indigenous Relations Committee members, but there was nowhere to place it in a communal area. I was proud of the accomplishments I had made and the progress of where Rotary was, but I knew there was still a lot of work to do. I was humbled and a bit embarrassed by all the pomp and ceremony, but I had to remind myself that I received this honour in the spirit of advancing Indigenous diversity and inclusion in Canada. I needed to use these fifteen minutes of "Rotary fame" to encourage others to take a learning and action journey. I spent the next six months giving local, regional, and international presentations to Rotarians.

In September, after the last one of these talks at the Waterton International Peace Park Conference, I was in my office doing some renovations when my elbow hit the shelf with the trophy. It went flying and crashed to the ground, breaking into hundreds of pieces. I was stunned to see this once-in-a-lifetime award shattered beyond recognition. As I swept it up and threw the broken pieces in the garbage, my family was mortified. But for some reason, I felt a weight off my shoulders. For me, it was some sort of relief not seeing it daily and reminding me that I was somehow embarrassed about receiving the trophy as a White man, as it was always meant for our collective efforts and accomplishments with and on behalf of building relationships with Indigenous people. The trophy was just a thing, but the meaning of the award and the title of Person of Action: Champion of Inclusion was a responsibility to the community and Rotary.

During this three-year process with Rotarians, I was able to put into practice the LIVE principles, with the Rotary culture. As Star Trek's Mr. Spock says, *"LIVE long and prosper."*

I **learned** about the politics, process, and principles of this group of people. Rotarians are well-meaning middle-aged people, the majority of which are male. Their culture and systems go back 119 years. They are "people of action" in their communities and leaders in business. Rotary is well known in many small towns and cities in Canada, but it is not well known for its works by younger generations and Indigenous peoples. Surprisingly, immigrants and new-comers to Canada have a positive perception of Rotary, as there are over forty-six thousand clubs around the world.

Having **integrity** was extremely important when working with Rotarians. They pride themselves with following their four-way test in all they think, say, or do:

- Is it the **truth**?
- Is it **fair** to all concerned?
- Will it build **goodwill** and better friendships?
- Will it be **beneficial** to all?

So, when I presented to leadership and members, I re-minded them of this oath and asked them to apply it to their relationships and dealings with Indigenous peoples. This oath was successful in helping them understand Indigenous ways of thinking and parallel systems of Rotary.

Valour was a strong factor in our success with Rotary. There were several times when I had to have heart-to-heart talks with district and club leaders about certain policies or practices. There was a heavy weight on my shoulders to make sure Rotary was following best practices and protocols when engaging with Indigenous peoples. My position was that if Indigenous issues were worth doing, they were worth doing right (long-term vision, commitment for many years, leadership support, and dedicated resources).

The **engagement** of Rotarians saw exponential growth, due to several factors. Many of them were waiting for Rotary to take an active role in the country's reconciliation process. Shortly after we started promoting the Rotary Indigenous Relations Committee, Canadians learned of the 751 unmarked graves found at a Kamloops-area Indian residential school. Rotarians wanted to learn more about Indigenous issues and identify opportunities for them and their clubs to support their local communities.

FOOD FOR THOUGHT:

1. When have you spent time learning about a community or racial group that is different from your own?

2. What can help motivate you to expand your understanding of people who are different from you in some significant way?

3. Does your organization have a set of values, and are they being upheld? How about their DIE values?

CHAPTER 21

IS IT TIME TO DIE?

THE DIE PENDULUM SWINGS WILDLY at times, and it often follows our political leanings from left to right and back again. Luckily, for the most part, Canadians in general see themselves as in the center, being socially progressive and caring about their fellow citizens while at the same time being fiscally conservative. With a few exceptions over the years, political parties have governed and put forward policies from the middle. In more recent years, the "Trump effect" has negatively influenced DIE initiatives in the United States and in Canada as well. Donald Trump's outspoken views of nativism and nationalism have inspired vocal minority politicians and business leaders to distance themselves from DIE. Several terms have been used to demonize DIE trends.

Political Correctness – This means choosing words that will not offend others, particularly in relation to their race, ethnicity, sexual orientation, and gender. I do not believe there is anything "political" about this. Why would we not want to use the correct and most updated terminology that people want to be known as? For instance, during the last thirty years, Indigenous community members self-identify with many names, including Indian, Native, Aboriginal, First Nations, Métis, and Inuit. It does not take a lot of research to learn the best words and may be as easy as respectfully asking people how they identify.

Woke – The word "Woke" has been used by African Americans since 1930 and was used more prolifically in the '60s, during the civil rights movement, in reference to being aware and awake of social justice and political issues. It has been used, mainly by the Black community and its allies, as a positive attribute of being informed and educated on social issues. In the last few years, American Conservative politicians have targeted wokeness and wokeism as a threat to mainstream rights and values. "Woke" is now synonymous and even more derogatory than the term "political correctness." I do not use the word "woke" or identify my work within it. I will let others do that if they wish.

Some people wonder if **affirmative action** is part of DIE. The answer is, not really. Affirmative action programs started in the United States in the 1960s due to the civil rights movement and legislation. Initially, it was created to address discrimination against Black individuals in the job market, including public service jobs, and in gaining acceptance into universities and colleges. Affirmative action did not arrive in Canada until the 1980s. In 1982, Section 15 of the Canadian Charter of Rights and Freedoms stated that all citizens are "to be treated with the same respect, dignity and consideration." Equality could be set aside by government programs aimed at "the improvement of conditions of disadvantaged individuals or groups including those that are disadvantaged because of race." The Charter permits but does not require affirmative action-type legislation.

In some cases in the US and Canada, affirmative action–type programs are involved in establishing quotas for Black students and non-White individuals in workplaces and universities. But here is the problem: These programs often resulted in those individuals being discriminated against as not being hired or enrolled in universities based on their merit, but rather just on their skin colour. So, ironically, to address discrimination, affirmative action ended up just creating a new opportunity to discriminate against people of colour. Some people even argue that affirmative action is extremely racist, as its premise is that certain groups cannot compete based on merit. This ignores the reality that some people who are highly qualified and have great merit are still passed over because of their race.

There is a common myth that affirmative action is prevalent in many fields. A surprising number of people think the only way you can get into policing is if you are female or from a visible minority group. When I go into a police recruit class or a criminal justice program and ask "Does affirmative action exist in law enforcement?" overwhelmingly everyone agrees. But when I ask them to look at their cohort, they see that White males make up 75 percent of the class. One of the problems with believing that affirmative action exists is that there then is an assumption that the people who get hired or promoted are there not due to their skills or knowledge, but because they are a "minority hire."

In recent years, affirmative action has been attacked by Conservatives on both sides of the border as favouring equity over equality. DIE has become more prevalent in workplaces, but DIE training has often been delivered in ways that are ineffective at best, and that turn people off from the whole concept of antiracism at worst.

LIVE Application

Take the time to **learn** about the history of DIE and what has been your organization's journey. You will see they have tried many things, called it different names, and had their share of successes and failures in the process. Timing is everything, so do your homework if you want to DIE successfully.

Integrity can be described as choosing between what is convenient and what is right. It may be easier to go with the flow of where the pendulum is, but that will not advance you or your organization. As Martin Luther said, "Every man must do two things alone; he must do his own believing and his own DIEing."

As a DIE advocate, you may feel you are on the wrong side of the pendulum, but have **valour** and be brave, as it will inevitably swing back. Sometimes bravery may mean stopping or pausing what you are doing and picking things up when timing is right for you and your organization. Time and history will be on your side.

One of my biggest lessons is to listen to and **engage** with others who do not think like me. This is hard, especially in our world of polarizing politics and social media targeting. I spend considerable time talking with and listening to people who have views that would be considered right wing or right of center. When I hear their concerns and arguments, it helps me develop common sense of rebuttals and focused arguments for the DIE case.

FOOD FOR THOUGHT:

1. When have you been in a job where the company DIE commitments were fully embraced by all the employees and the C-suite leaders? What was the culture organizational culture like?

2. Why do you think many companies struggle to implement DIE?

CHAPTER 22

*TO DIE OR NOT TO DIE – THAT IS
THE CORPORATE QUESTION.*

MOST ORGANIZATIONS, WHETHER THEY ARE corporate, government, or non-profit, are led by humans (boards, presidents, CEOs, or executive directors), staffed by humans (managers, team leaders, full-time and part-time staff), supported by humans (donors, volunteers, contractors), or they provide services to humans (customers, clients, community). As such, the first and sometimes only point of contact they have with DIE is with their human resources departments and people.

If you have looked for a job recently, you may have noticed that when companies post job openings, they provide a paragraph about the company and a description of the job duties and requirements, and they close with a DIE statement. Here is an example:

Critical Mass is an equal opportunity employer that is committed to diversity and inclusion in the workplace. We do not tolerate discrimination based on race, national origin, gender, gender identity, sexual orientation, protected veteran status, disability, age, or other legally protected status. If you are an individual with disabilities who would like to request an accommodation, please reach out to accommodations@criticalmass.com.

We are committed to fostering diversity, equity, and inclusion within our candidate pools.

Companies also include diversity statements on their websites, often as part of their mission statement. Here are examples from BMW and Peel Region:

BMW

Headline: "Joy through diversity"

Diversity strengthens our company. The diverse input of our colleagues from over 110 countries makes us who we are: A Bavarian automotive brand that is at home in the world. Diversity – in all its forms – is one of the most important success factors for us. Because just as diverse our customers, suppliers, investors and partners worldwide are, so diverse are our teams, who manage to put a smile on the faces of our customers every day.

Passion knows no differences. This is why we encourage diversity in all our teams. Because if you want to set standards in shaping the sustainable and individual mobility of the future, you also have to go ahead with the corporate culture. This diversity in our teams enables us to better understand, reflect and make more intelligent decisions about the various requirements of our stakeholders from all over the world. Our diversity is the cornerstone of our company's success and not only secures our innovative strength, but also our long-term competitiveness.

Our commitment to more diversity. To us, equal opportunities and inclusion are a lived reality, not an empty promise – every day and everywhere. Because the different and complementary perspectives and abilities of everyone increase our innovative power and make us strong for any challenge.

Multifaceted insights. The promotion of tolerance, inclusion, equal opportunities, and active action against any form of discrimination are crucial for us in the further development of our culture and our mindset. We hold numerous Diversity, Equity, and Inclusion Days (DEI Days) annually, where important topics are addressed and explored in depth together with our talents on selected international action days.

Peel Region

Headline: "Diversity, equity, and inclusion. Creating a diverse and inclusive Peel"

Peel Region strives to build a community in which residents and staff enjoy a sense of belonging, regardless of income, race, gender, or social status.

We're committed to:

- Ensuring all residents are treated fairly and have access to programs and services.
- Working with our residents to deliver programs and services that are not only inclusive and equitable, but also reflective of our communities.

We'll achieve this by:

- Removing systemic barriers and addressing racism.
- Adopting an intentional approach to equity in programming and service delivery.

For a better understanding of our commitment to creating a diverse and inclusive culture, read our Five-Year DEI Strategy, 2025-2029.

Diversity, Inclusion, and Equity statements are great if they are implemented consistently. Even the best policies and intentions fail when individual biases or corporate procedures short-circuit the process by not going beyond platitudes and social media posts.

A role of any human resources (HR) department is to develop processes to attract, retain, and advance the best candidates for the jobs. With changing demographics, HR specialists must look at their past practices, revise them, and include DIE strategies to expand their reach and impact.

As a consultant to a major oil and gas company in Canada, one of the questions I asked was how it hired summer students and interns. Immediately I was told that it used the age-old system of employee referrals. Now, this may not have been an issue, if not for the fact that most of the managers and staff were of European descent (White) and male. In my reports to them, I noted that many people who are hired in these roles are more likely to get full-time opportunities, as the organization gets a chance to vet the student, and the student builds a relationship with the staff and managers. By not opening these opportunities to others, they are limiting their pool of future candidates. Recent studies have found that applicants who were referred were four-and-a-half more times likely to get hired than those who did not have a connection to the organization. After noting several flaws like this in their recruitment and hiring systems, they took my reports and did nothing. Not surprisingly, I was not hired for any further consultations with them.

While supporting the Calgary Police Service's recruiting unit, I held several outreach engagement events with them in the Muslim, Sikh, and Black communities. It was shocking to hear that their youth had the perception that our officers hated them, and they would not be welcomed in the department. I reflected on these comments and recalled that some police officers did not like or trust people from ethnocultural communities. This inspired me to work harder to get better representation from demographics that we had very little on the job, if any. I noticed that once we were able to get more Muslim and Sikh officers, perceptions started to change. Neither the police nor the community could negatively generalize or stereotype the other. As the saying goes, "If you point one finger, there are three more pointing back at you." Now, for example, Muslims could not say that all police were prejudiced against them, because one of their brother Muslims was a cop. Likewise, police could not generalize Muslims as criminals, as there were some of them among their ranks.

Organizational Fit – Code Words for Discrimination

After all the rhetoric of being a welcoming and inclusive employer, HR staff and managers must review hundreds of applications. Due to the volume, they are weeding out people using certain criteria that they have set. These criteria must meet bonified occupational requirements (BFOR) to pass any human rights concerns. This means that successful candidates can perform the job effectively and safely. What workplaces often do not do well is weed in DIE skills and attributes, looking to the future benefit of the organization. Once candidates make it to the interview stages, questions should be asked like, "Have you worked with a culture that is different from yours?" or "Describe how your career has been enhanced by exposure to diverse people, places, or experiences."

While sitting on an interview panel several years ago, we had an interviewee of Southeast Asian descent, from Korea. The police candidate took at least ten seconds after every question to answer. In the debrief with the panel, a senior officer said he was uncomfortable with the candidate, as he felt he was lying or making up the answers. I rebutted that people from his culture take more time to respond to questions or make statements, as they do not want to lose face or put their foot in their mouth, as our culture may do. He was not convinced, and after much debate he said he did not think he could work in a patrol car with this individual and might not be a good fit. I again challenged the officer's assumptions, and the HR specialist on the panel did not back me. That officer came up to me several weeks afterwards and was upset that I made him look bad, stating I would pay for it later.

LIVE Application

It is important to **learn** about best practices as well as promising principles. Best practices are those working programs, initiatives, and solutions that have proven track records, while promising principles are the underlying reasons why they are successful. For instance, the best practice could be the organization setting measurable DIE goals. The principle is that if DIE goals are measured and leaders are asked to report on them, they will get done.

For DIE to be successful, the organization must be behind it. The HR staff, managers, and frontline need to believe that their **integrity** will be supported when they propose DIE initiatives and if they challenge the status quo that conflicts with it.

Your **valour** will be tested in advancing DIE. Change is difficult for many people, especially if it challenges their worldview and they feel resistance is futile.

Star Trek's Q once said, "It's not safe out here. It's wondrous, with treasures to satiate desires both subtle and gross; but it's not for the timid."

Look to **engage** with people who are in the same sector doing similar DIE work. There are meet-up groups, online and in person, where you can connect, compare, and commiserate. Also, many organizations have affinity groups that bring together people of similar backgrounds or identities to advance and implement DIE strategies.

FOOD FOR THOUGHT:

1. In your work and social circles, what shifts in attitudes have occurred towards the growth of immigrant populations in our communities? How about Indigenous people, 2SLGBTQ+, or people with disabilities?

2. How does your workplace or organization reflect the true diversity of your community?

CHAPTER 23

MALE, PALE AND STALE
– WHAT IS NEXT?

LIVE LIKE YOU ARE DIEING

EVERYONE UNDERSTANDS THAT WITH THE changing demographics in our society now and going forward, DIE work is a business and social imperative. Population demographic data show that Indigenous people, people of colour, and newcomer communities are growing at a faster rate than the general population. Between 2016 and 2021, the Indigenous population grew by 9.4 percent, which is the largest community by natural birth, and in 2023, 97.6 percent of Canada's population growth was because of immigration. For business, this means customers, investors, and employee pools are different than they were twenty years ago and will look significantly different ten years from now.

For some nonprofits and the voluntary sector, it is going to be an even more striking difference, as they are late to the game and have been most resistant to the changes in society. This is already occurring in many nonprofits that were founded by people of European ancestry and built their base with only this demographic profile. As the White population is shrinking, North American nonprofit organizations are losing the opportunities to attract members, donors, and even clients with which they do not identify.

As they say in business, "If you don't grow, you die," but I would argue that if you embrace DIE, you will grow (beyond your wildest expectations). Most organizations start seeing the writing on wall when it is too late. Their numbers are sliding, they are unable to retain people, there is an increase in internal discrimination and human rights complaints, or there is a crisis in the community like the death of George Floyd or the finding of children's graves at Indian residential schools.

There is a management saying, "If you can't measure it—you can't manage it." A difficult part of the problem for organizations jumping into diversity initiatives is that they may go in with their heart only and not have the insight to start sustainable change. Proactive initiatives are some of the most challenging to measure, but they are the most important. In policing, some things can be easily measured, such as the number of calls for service, crimes committed, investigations conducted, and suspects charged. It is much more difficult for law enforcement to ascertain how many people did not become a victim of a crime or how many individuals were diverted from engaging in criminal activities.

Before getting engaged in any diversity initiative, the organization needs to explore what its current leader, staff, donor, and client demographics are. This baseline data can start with subjective observations, but it should lead to data obtained directly from these stakeholders. It is only after you obtain this information that you can draft and implement a plan. But do not wait for the perfect plan. There are some best practices, but each initiative needs to be tailored to the environment and organization. A challenge in this work is measuring and identifying contributions against attribution. For instance, shortly after starting the Rotary Indigenous strategy in 2021, there was a huge increase in members wanting to learn more about Indigenous issues and how they could support members in that community. You could infer that this was due to the resources and personnel being available, but it was more than likely due to the national dialogue that followed the discovery of the 215 unmarked graves at the Kamloops Indian Residential School in 2021.

LIVE Application

An important step in your journey is to do the homework. **Learn** about the community by undertaking open source/Google research. Find out the demographics, history, and current events of the people you are working with and for. Investigate best practices and promising DIE principles for your sector and those being done in others.

"You know the greatest danger facing us is ourselves, and irrational fear of the unknown. There is no such thing as the unknown. Only things temporarily hidden, temporarily not understood."

—Captain Kirk

DIE work is like no other. It requires the values of **integrity** to start it and a commitment to integrate it into all aspects of the organization. The outcomes and progress must be documented and celebrated. You need to be honest with yourself and others so that this work is not "flavour of month" or "one and done."

Organization leaders must be brave and have **valour** as they champion DIE work. There are lots of naysayers who have power in the intuitions and are resistant to change. These vocal minorities can disrupt and derail DIE changes.

Engaging with internal and external stakeholders will help identify where the barriers and opportunities are to advance DIE. Again, this, like all system change, takes time to do. As philosopher Lao Tsu said, "A journey of a thousand miles begins with a single step."

FOOD FOR THOUGHT:

1. Are you ready to be a DIE Champion in your community or workplace?

2. How much time and effort are you prepared to devote to the LIVE actions?

CHAPTER 24

CONCLUSION

I HOPE THIS BOOK HAS BEEN as enjoyable to read as it has been for me to write. Sharing my DIE journey through storytelling, jokes, and some of my favourite quotes has been a fun process that has helped me uncover some of my own motivations, biases, and struggles. I am sure that anyone who has gone through this kind of process can understand both the cathartic relief of sharing their story as well as the fear of opening old wounds and struggles. As you can see by my diverse experiences, my path has not been a straightforward one. Author Kathy Boyd Fellure accurately pointed out that "The joy is in the journey, the struggle is part of the joy, and the final destination is not an end but another beginning of another journey."

The LIVE acronym for Learn, Integrity, Valour and Engagement can be a life lesson to follow outside of DIE. In developing this simple template, I believe leaders, HR specialists, DIE practitioners, and advocates can easily advance their organizations and communities to welcome more diverse people, have inclusive policies and processes, and offer more equitable opportunities for all.

One of my favourite songs, "Live Like You Were Dying" by Tim McGraw, has a strong message of living today fully and having no regrets. My hope is that all who read this book will aspire to lead their families, friends, and colleagues to LIVE it up!

ACKNOWLEDGMENTS

It has been a huge challenge to condense over forty years of living DIE into a book that will be useful for people from many backgrounds and sectors. As I mentioned in the previous chapters, I have not and could not have been successful doing this alone. If I could, I would list all the folks in my life and career who have inspired me, shared their stories, and taught me life lessons, but that would be a 40-page novel in itself. (Ha—maybe that's my next book!) I started this book by dedicating it "To all my relations," meaning in short, to family (past, present, and future) and the universe that we are all connected to. I will finish it that way as well but needed to express appreciation to those who contributed to creating this book.

I am deeply grateful to my family for their unwavering support throughout this journey. To my spouse, Marina, who was my rock and second set of eyes through the countless hours of writing and revisions, and to my mom, Delia, and daughters, Jessica and Connie, who were my constant cheerleaders and inspiration through the process. I am so blessed to have had constant love and support of my sons, Jason, Noel, and Tim, as well as my sons-in-law, Farouq and Miles, and daughters-in-law, Karen and Marcella. My work has been inspired by my grandchildren, Adam, Anthony, Izabelle, Kingston, Maria Jose, Maxwell, Nicholas, Sofia, Valentina, who I hope they and their generation will manage to DIE better then we have.

I want to express gratitude to Doug Jones, my brother from another mother, who encouraged me by providing feedback and ideas for the book.

In appreciation of the guidance and wisdom provided by Elder Dr. Doreen Spence, one cup of tea at a time, as well as continual prayers in between.

Special thanks to my friend Derrick Shirley, who inspired me to start and finish my book writing journey. His pointed questions forced me to dive deeper into self-discovery than I was originally imagining doing in the writing process.

I am thankful for the expertise of Richelle Wiseman of Inscape Communications, for her invaluable assistance in editing the manuscript and pushing my written skills.

Heartfelt thanks to Susan Coombes, Christopher Kane, Andrea Sabah, Jessica Stewart, and Donna Aziz, whose constructive criticism (as they always do so well) strengthened the narrative and substance of the book.

Additionally, I am grateful that I found a wonderful artist, Hasanka Naleen, to add entertaining graphics to bring life to the book's content.

Last, but not least, thanks to Roger Brooks and everyone on the American Real Publishing Team who helped me so much to bring this book across the finish line. A special thanks to Debra Hartmann, the ever-patient Chief Publishing Officer, and Roger Harvey for the greatest cover design I could ever imagine.

ABOUT THE AUTHOR

Cam grew up within a large extended Lebanese family where he learned to appreciate his ancestry while navigating Canadian discrimination towards it. After spending 25 years with the Calgary Police Service, he continued his DIE journey, where he has worked for the Alberta Human Rights Commission and many organizations seeking equity.

Cam has been gifted the Blackfoot name of *Mikotsapinukum*, meaning Red Morning, for his years of service to the Indigenous community, which he proudly and humbly carries in his work. He has spent several decades as a strong advocate and leader of DIE initiatives, training, strategies, and programs, as well as an international speaker in the field.

Cam has been the recipient of numerous awards, including Jewish Repairing the World Award, YMCA Peace Medal, Baha'i Community Racial Harmony Award, the Alberta Outstanding Contribution to Community Adult Learning Award, and the Calgary Police Service Chief's

Award for Community Service. Under his leadership and guidance, the Calgary Police Service received the Calgary Immigrant Aid Society's Immigrant of Distinction Corporate Diversity Award and the Federation of Canadian Municipalities Diversity Award. While board chair for 12 CSI and the Alberta Hate Crimes Committee, the organizations received Alberta Community Justice Awards. In 2023, Rotary International acknowledged Cam as a Person of Action: Champion of Inclusion, and that same year, he was presented with the Queen's Platinum Jubilee Medal by the Province of Alberta.

With a master's in Intercultural Communication, he has advised hundreds of corporations, non-profit organizations, and all orders of governments in developing equitable practices and removing barriers for all people. Cam is the president and founder of Kanata Intercultural Consulting.

WEBSITE

NOTE FROM THE AUTHOR:

If you are interested in having me speak at an event or present a workshop, you can reach me here: cam@camstewart.net

If you are interested in signing up for my newsletter or learning more about how I can help you with your DIE journey, please go to my website at https://camstewart.net/

I am happy to share my experience and insights with individuals and groups seeking to create a greater sense of diversity, inclusion, and equity in their communities and workforces. It is my hope that my struggles and successes in the DIE will be a support and inspiration for your journey. Feel free to contact me if you have any questions or would like to share your achievements in this field.

Let's connect on social media:

To keep connected with me as I continue my DIE journey, feel free to follow my travels on:

LinkedIn – linkedin.com/in/camstewartyyc

Facebook – facebook.com/camstewartyyc

YouTube – youtube.com/@livetodietoday

Let's DIE together!

In service and with heart,
Cam Stewart (Mikotsapinukum)

OTHER PUBLICATIONS
BY CAM STEWART

Ngo, H.V., Rossiter, M.J., Stewart, C. (2011). "Crime and crime prevention in a multicultural society." Calgary: Centre for Criminology and Justice Research.

> Looks at the current perceptions and realities of crime prevention initiatives and their effectiveness with ethnocultural communities. The research provides insight into the risks and protective factors of our immigrant communities and suggestions for proactive crime prevention strategies.

Stewart, C. (2007). "Combating Hate and Bias Crime and Incidents in Alberta: Current responses and recommendations for the future." Calgary.

> Studies the current national and international trends and strategies that are being used to respond to hate crime and compares this to the experiences of vulnerable communities within Alberta. The research and findings articulate the need for appropriate prevention and enforcement responses.

Pruegger, V., Stewart C. and Jones, D. (2004). "Young People and Policing: Meeting the Challenge of Diversity Together." Ottawa: RCMP.

Looks at the experiences and initiatives of policing agencies in working with young people to identify strategies for mutual trust and cooperation around discrimination and hate activity. Makes recommendations and presents recommendations made by youth themselves.

Pruegger. V., Stewart C. and Jones, D. (2004). "Community Policing in the 21st Century: Creating National and International Linkages." Ottawa: Canadian Heritage.

Explores barriers to developing community policing, highlights advantages of pursuing partnerships between communities and police agencies, in particular between diverse communities and local police.